THE
'CELLIST
INNER
VOICE

Ian Bewley

ISBN 1 897927 03 7
© Ian Bewlay, Watermillock-on-Ullswater, England.
Published by Da Capo Music Ltd.,
Carrington House, 92, New Road, HEDON, E. Yorks, HU12 8BS England.
Tel; 0482 890008

26 Stanway Road
Whitefield
Manchester
M45 8EG

A CIP catalogue record for this book is available from the British Library.

ISBN 1 897927 03 7

Dedicated to the memory of VILMOS PALOTAI,
a musician and 'cellist of rare talent
and deep musical insight.

CONTENTS

The 'Cellist's Inner Voice

Foreword

Ian Bewley is one of those people whose entire life evolves through music. When he is not teaching or playing, he is listening to it. High quality music reproducing equipment has always fascinated him and his collection of discs is formidable. Our association is long and deep. I can see him now, taking copious notes at my courses in Cumbria year after year followed by questions and discussions on our long walks among the mountains. His impeccable artistic integrity and insatiable curiosity about all aspects of music-making was always inspiring. He appreciates the awesome responsibility of teaching a stringed instrument: that aches and pains caused by playing can ruin the magic of music and cause great mental anguish. He knows that the function of a teacher is to be able to prevent tension and anxiety by highlighting structured physical and mental exercises, and by being able to demonstrate that the unification of mind, body and spirit can co-ordinate the natural balances into an effortless and powerful whole.

This book is long overdue and I cannot think of anyone else who could translate the principles of the "New Approach" for 'cellists better than Ian. I endorse and recommend it whole-heartedly.

Kató Havas, Oxford, 1993.

Author's Notes

The writing of this book could have said to have begun at 6.30 p.m. on Monday, February 16th, 1948 at a recital by the Hungarian Quartet - Zoltan Szekely, Alexandre Moskowsky, Denes Koromzay and Vilmos Palotai - at the Manchester Chamber Concerts Society.

The shock of this kind of musical experience only happens once in a lifetime. It was my first exposure to an entirely new approach to music, demonstrating a unique sublety with tremendous power.

I knew that from then on I would not rest until I had discovered what it was that made it possible to communicate music with such overwhelming power which seemed to come directly from the composer.

A few years later, circumstances made it possible for me to go to Switzerland to study with Vilmos Palotai. He had retired from the quartet and had formed the Hungarian (Piano) Trio.

I will always be grateful for his patience and help. Musically, his mind was like quicksilver; his knowledge, ability and experience vast. It was an "open sesame".

On enquiring from whence came such authority, he said, "As a young man of 19 in Berlin there were, readily available in the libraries, the (Beethoven) sketch books - the autograph scores, you know!"

I asked why he was in Berlin. "I was in the Philharmoniker for a while", he said. It was a fair assumption that he would be the principal 'cello, but he said "No, I was number three". "Who then", I asked, "occupied the first desk?" "Emanuel Feuermann and Gregor Piatigorsky", he replied.

Imagine the situation; two of the finest 'cellists the world has ever known, and in Feuermann's case, most 'cellists including Casals would agree, without question *the* finest, along with a 'cellist who was to become a giant in the field of chamber music, to be all together for a short period in the 'cello section of an orchestra.

This is a pointer to the fact that in whatever field of music we find ourselves, ideally the process of musical thinking and working should always be the same whether it be as a soloist, a chamber music player, or an orchestral player.

However, it is not an ideal world, and particularly in this age, there are tremendous pressures on all aspects of music-making due to lack of rehearsal time, poor conditions and financial constraints.

For the soloist and the chamber music player it is possible to call a halt to recharge the batteries from time to time. But it is not quite as easy to achieve this respite in an orchestra. The mental, and consequently, the physical pressures build up very quickly causing the inevitable feeling of being trapped.

I hope that some of the suggestions in this book may help to release this feeling and bring back the joy of making music.

If I were asked to give a musical example of what this book represents, I would say "Hear the Hungarian Trio's recording of Beethoven's Op70 no.1, (The Ghost) and in particular the cry from the 'cello's tenor register shortly after the opening of the slow movement, where words are not only inadequate but totally super-fluous".

Unfortunately, these recordings are not generally available at present, but I hope that EMI in France may be persuaded to re-issue them as they did for the Hungarian Quartet's recording of the Beethoven cycle, for which they are to be warmly congratulated.

Many of the allusions in this book are Palotai's, and I can only hope they have not become distorted in the telling.

Early in 1960, a friend lent my wife and me a book called "A New Approach to Violin Playing" by Kató Havas. It only took us a few seconds to recognise that here were the fundamental principles that I had been discovering from Vilmos Palotai.

Kató Havas, as a very young girl at the Budapest Academy, was a pupil and protegée of Imre Waldbauer, the first violin of the original Hungarian Quartet, whose mantle had fallen on the quartet I heard in 1948. The connection was obvious!

Very soon after reading the book, we studied with Kató Havas as a quartet and ever since, the "New Approach" has been part of my life, so naturally this book is based on the principles of her teaching as they apply to the 'cello. It could be said that I have copied large sections from her books, especially "Stage Fright", but because of my connection with this teaching over thirty years, it is inevitable that this would seem to be so.

The "New Approach" has become so much a part of the way I teach that consequently Kató Havas has been extremely generous and understanding in allowing me to use her ideas and terminology in this book.

In her workshops she has been known to say, when participants get the message too much mixed up with the messenger, "It is not me, it is *it*". This *it* is the universal and powerful flow of music.

I can say with equal confidence, "it is not me, it is *them*", *them* being Vilmos Palotai and Kató Havas. Most of the ideas in this book are theirs, not mine, and I am sure that both of them would agree that their ideas stem from fundamental principles and truths.

Not only am I grateful to Kató Havas for allowing me to use her ideas, but also for helping me personally in a tremendously practical way in making it possible for me to put forward these ideas in public, both as a performer and teacher. I know of many violinists and violists who have suffered from even greater problems than my own, who owe Kató Havas a great debt of gratitude for giving them back their musical lives and careers.

I am sure that they would wish to join me in saying a big "thank you".   ,

I should like to thank my first teacher, Leonard Baker, an artist who gave me such a good start and implanted in me the right attitude to music., also my thanks go to Dr. Ben Horsfall for many hours of patience, and much humour, in helping me with harmony, counterpoint and music generally.

Frederic Cox, the last Principal of the Royal Manchester College of Music was always supportive, giving me the opportunity to play chamber music, and encouraging me to find a teacher who eventually turned out to be Vilmos Palotai, for which I was most grateful.

My thanks to my pupils, past and present, and in particular to one who has a hearing loss and who was able to take Grade 8 of the ABRSM successfully without the adjudicator realizing that the candidate was unable to hear normally - indeed this demonstrated to me, in a very practical way, that music is much more than just what we hear with normal hearing!

Acknowledgements

In addition to those mentioned in the Author's Notes, I should like to thank the following, without whom this project could not have happened:-

To Edition Delrieu of Nice for their kind permission to quote from their publication "60 Etudes du Jeune Violoncelliste" by Feuillard.

To Michael and Denyse Simcock for all the photographs. Also to Mrs. Dalton for typing the initial drafts and to Mrs. Jean Allison for typing and copying the subsequent work.

To Nick Bibby, for the cover illustration.

To Da Capo Music Ltd., the publishers.

To my brother, Edmund, for his literary and scientific advice, and last but not least, my gratitude to my wife Dorothy, whose commitment to music, encouragement and patience made it all possible.

Ian Bewley
Watermillock, 1993.

Introduction

Fritz Kreisler's last words to his audience in the Carnegie Hall on his retirement were "If I have any one regret, it is that, in our present mechanical age, the growing generations of musicians may never be able to experience that indescribable, intangible something that made the profession of musicians so beautiful and satisfying in my time and age".

Nothing is for ever. Like life itself we are not able to hang on to or hold on to anything including our children, our animals, or our own lives. We are part of a constant flow of which music is a powerful part. It is through music that it is possible to glimpse the nature of life in that kaleidoscopic, fascinating vibration.

That "indescribable, intangible something" is surely the uninhibited joy of the communication of those vibrations.

Kreisler's "regret" is only too audible today; extremely talented and competent musicians who do not find that "indescribable, intangible something" can be heard in profusion. Those few who can give us "The Magic" cannot be denied. They demand that you must listen to them; their spell is so strong.

Is it possible for us to find the way to Kreisler's "indescribable, intangible something" now?

The "New Approach to Violin Playing" by Kató Havas, for those who have the courage to accept its message, will show the way. Courage, because we may have the awareness to recognise the truth in the "New Approach" but because of outside pressures, previous training, the way we have to earn a living, and the way we view ourselves, we do not feel able to put it into practice. The fact that we understand this may help us to have the courage.

What is "New"?

It could be said that there is nothing new in some of the ideas in "The New Approach". What is new is their organisation into an organic whole. Indeed, as the reader becomes attuned to the ideas they may recognise that they belong to universal principles pervading all life; the organisation of these principles for the specific use of violinists and violists is most certainly new.

Violinists received immediate help when Kató Havas, the author of "A New Approach to Violin Playing", began teaching in the early 1960s. All those who needed help because they were suffering from varying degrees of discomfort, found new hope when they learned how to use the fundamental balances of the body in order to release tension. When this took place the sonority they were able to produce took on a new dimension and their potential had no limit!

As her teaching inevitably grew and developed she realised that most violinists (and musicians in general) have not had the benefit of the grounding that nearly all Hungarian children have in music as of right; that is, they are first of all taught to clap to the pulse and sing the intervals in order to develop and nurture their inner feeling for the music. Only when the inner strength of the music is great enough is the child guided towards a particular instrument. Ideally this should be followed up by imaginative teaching in order to allow the child's imagination to blossom and to appreciate the musical drama in pulse and interval, otherwise even this process can become dull and mechanical.

The previous paragraph encapsulates the framework for future creative practice which most aspiring musicians and instrumentalists will certainly find new, perhaps not entirely in the basic idea, but mainly to the degree to which first of all it is necessary to work inwardly and only after that is done, to discover the music through the instrument. The normal predicament is to be put to a particular instrument and somehow pick up music on the way; rather like expecting to become an artist by using those traced-out numbered shapes on paper with colour instructions on each. Painting by numbers!

So we see a central idea of the "New Approach" is that music comes from "inside-out"; that is, the individual is a transmitter through which the music is able to flow via the instrument to the listener.

"Stage Fright" is the book which follows "A New Approach" and "The Twelve Lesson Course", encapsulating all the previous ideas in the two former works but going more deeply into the psychological problems of the violinist wherein lie the source of tension.

The subject discussed in "Stage Fright" is vast but the solution to the problem is simple and specific. We feel the urge to have to work hard physically, but the realisation that we have to do so little, comparatively, is very difficult to accept. Our chief problem *is* to accept its simplicity and to act on it. From this grows another seemingly contradictory idea — "Never try to play beautifully". Seemingly this goes against everything we are supposed to strive for. Surely to play beautifully is the goal of every musician, particularly the 'cellist? A deeper look into the problem will help us to understand that if we strive hard to play beautifully and to please our listeners our ego is automatically taking charge with the result that tension is generated in a snowball effect and often, the meaning of the music is forgotten.

Simply then, if we put the music first from "inside-out" the music itself will dictate its quality and we will be too involved in doing what we have to do to produce it to generate tension worrying if it is beautiful or not. A classic example is the true Hungarian Gypsy violinist (fiddler) whose only aim in life is to give you the music!

Obviously there is a great deal more to be said about these ideas before they can be of practical use, but they must certainly rank as "new".

Why Approach?

In this connotation "approach" means "a way towards" or "a continuous search". The definition has a connection with the nature of music itself, that is, an ever-flowing movement in time into which the player tunes himself to act as a transmitter. In order to do this he must put his own ego to one side as it is for the nature of the music that he must search.

Whatever has been achieved today does not happen tomorrow as of right; it has to be re-created each time.

"Let's find out what happens" is a theme which runs through the "New Approach" as opposed to learning certain laid-down skills which is the way of nearly all "Methods". A "Method", and there are many good ones, in this connotation is the opposite of an approach. Method suggests something fixed, immutable, whereas approach is a way, a search, finding out what happens. This in no way means a "free-for-all". During the search we will discover very specific and detailed things we will have to do, and later on when it comes to learning repertoire the utmost discipline will be required.

So we can say that a method usually goes the mechanical way from "outside-in". This means that we translate what we see on the music paper to certain laid down actions on our instrument and hope that music is the result. On the other hand an "Approach" suggests that we translate what we see on the written page, or music we already "know" to an inner knowledge or process. Initially this is done by clapping the pulse and singing the intervals to the note names; the "Inside-out" process.

It will be seen that as this approach unfolds, anything that is fixed, static or "safe" is anti-music, but anything that has the possibility of movement or change is part of the musical process.

Can the "New Approach" help the 'cellist?

Whatever works for the violinist works for all the other string players and any other instrumentalist as well. As we have said, the principles involved are universal and can be applied to any activity if done with true understanding.

Superficially there seem to be many differences between the violinist and the 'cellist. The first is the obvious one of size and the necessity of the 'cellist always to be seated with the instrument presented to the body in a different direction. However, we shall see that thinking of the body balances, a violinist seated in orchestra or chamber ensemble, should have identical body posture in balance to that of the 'cellist. The working of both arms and hands in relation to each instrument is identical, as will be seen.

There may be certain barriers built up in 'cellists' thinking that could make it difficult for certain sections of "The New Approach" to be accepted, simply because 'cellists have never done it before. The thumb connection with bow-stick and hair is a specific point, and we will deal with the practicality in context. However, the ideal is not to search for what is deemed "right" but what is "true" and works. If the true use of the connection between right hand and bow with the use of a balanced right arm releases any sign of tension and produces a better sonority than ever before, why worry that it has not been done like that before?

The truth running through the "New Approach" like a golden thread is that music is composed of the pulse and intervals and to produce music we must have this pulse and interval within ourselves. We could call them collectively "The Inner Pulse Song", but it is on the degree to which we must have this inner pulse song within us that we must concentrate.

Unfortunately for most of us the inner pulse song is like a tiny pale plant covered by heaps of rubble, never seeing the light of day. Our first work then is to scrape away the debris, letting in light and air, allowing the plant to grow and flourish. When the inner pulse song has become strong enough within ourselves, nurtured by our own musical imagination we are more than half way to solving the problem of how to communicate it to the outside world. The more strongly we feel the inner pulse song, the more strongly we feel the desire to communicate it.

How we can co-ordinate ourselves physically with the 'cello to produce our inner pulse song to the outside world is what we hope to discover in the following chapters.

Chapter 1

The Physical Aspects

As it is not possible to make music without movement, our first problem is physical inhibition which is brought about by misinterpreted impressions from the sense of sight and touch regarding written music and the feel of the 'cello itself.

The solution is to organise our thoughts, feelings and actions into a co-ordinated whole, and the first work in this organisation is to develop the pulse in the whole of our being.

It is significant that at all stages of our musical development, the basic and fundamental work is done first without an instrument.

Stand with the feet slightly apart to feel completely balanced with your arms hanging loosely by your sides. Swing up the arms into a clapping position and to any appropriate tune with a swing in it that you choose to sing, clap the pulse. If you are clapping in an entirely natural and free way you will notice that not only do your arms swing, but the whole of your body is involved. Also you will find that your knees will give slightly as a natural part of the whole movement.

The arms should swing in a natural circular movement with the hands coming together opposite the chest and springing upwards and apart in front of the face to come round again for the next clap. This natural clapping allows energy flow to take place involving the whole body which sends the song on the pulse from "inside-out". However, if we just bring the hands together with a straight horizontal movement of the arms, this just produces a mechanical dead "beat" which, like polite and dutiful applause, is an "outside-in" activity.

When you feel that you have the singing and clapping as naturally as breathing, vary the quality from *forte* to *piano* and back again. You will find that there is a *forte* energy and a *piano* energy rather than just a louder and more active singing and clapping for *forte*, and a quieter and less active singing and clapping for *piano*.

Already we are learning tone production through the power of the imagination!

Being self-conscious of either having an inadequate voice or just looking plain foolish are two excuses often put forward for not doing this exercise. As it is at the very heart of music-making and achieving the "inside-out" experience, who minds airing a poor quality voice or looking foolish as long as the meaning of the music is communicated and produces positive results?

It is surprising how the quality of the voice improves, even without formal training as this exercise becomes second nature and is produced with joy and imagination!

It is almost impossible to express in words the nature and importance of the strength and energy in this all-pervasive pulse. It is the life force of music without which all else is of little significance and a few minutes in the company of someone who has it to a degree will be enough to demonstrate the necessity of its acquisition and development for successful music making of any kind. It is also possible that teachers who are gifted with a powerful pulse are not always aware of their gift and assume that everyone else is so gifted. That is why sometimes it is possible for a teacher to miss the main factor in a pupil's development.

Discovering the Balances

As in the previous exercise, stand with the feet slightly apart to be balanced, throw the arms up and allow them to fall in front of the chest allowing the forearms, wrists and hands to be suspended naturally, rather like a bear looks when it stands on its hind legs to beg for food (see Plate. 1). The wrists will flex naturally allowing the fingers, which will be curved naturally, to point to the floor.

The feeling to develop is that the large back and shoulder muscles "suspend" the arms allowing them to swing gently on the shoulder joints. The arms are now like two gates swinging easily on their oiled hinges and could be moved by the lightest puff of wind. Imagine shoulder seams of whatever garment you are wearing to be the hinges on which the gates (your arms) can swing freely.

It is most important to understand and to experience the difference between allowing the arms to hang and suspending the arms. If the arms are hung you will feel their weight but if they are suspended they will be weightless.

To endorse the positive feeling of freedom when the true arm balance is achieved, it is a good idea to grip the thumbs against the fingers to feel how the muscles underneath the forearm tighten to lock the elbow joints, then release the grip to feel the freedom in the elbow joints once more.

Again, in the arm balanced position, draw up the naturally hanging hands to the horizontal by straightening the wrists and feel how the muscles on the upper part of the upper arms lock the shoulder joints, then release the wrists, allowing the hands to hang again in order to feel the freedom in the shoulder joints.

The large strong muscles in the back and shoulders are responsible for the weightless condition of the arms and can be compared to the counterbalance weight of a gramophone pick-up arm which allows the exact amount of weight and tracking force through the stylus into the groove of the record. The analogy is that the balanced right arm will produce the natural opening and swing which will produce an effortless bow stroke and, along with the "connection" with the right hand, which we will go into in great detail later, will help to produce the most desirable feeling that "there is no bow", just a balanced swing of the right arm. The balance in the left arm will allow complete freedom of movement for the left hand so that the all-important spaces between the knuckles are free to produce the musical intervals. These specific aspects will be treated in great detail later and are only mentioned now to demonstrate how important it is to discover the fundamental balances in the shoulders and arms in this early stage of development.

Use the previous pulsing exercise to discover the arm balances but instead of clapping, allow the arms to swing on their hinges to the pulse. It is important to realise that the arms are allowed to swing in balance on the momentum of their own weight with only the slightest initial motivation and not to "pump" them backwards and forwards with a conscious movement. Perhaps it would be a good idea to choose a gentle tune at first for the arm balance exercise to obviate the tendency to overdo the arm movements. We will put the arm balances to practical use when we have discussed the posture.

However, before we do this we should experience another associated exercise. This is the "Flip-flop" or rather the "Flop-flip".

As we said at the start of this section when we were discovering the arm balances, the wrists just hang naturally allowing the hand and fingers to point to the floor: this is the "Flop" position. Now rotate your arms upwards and outwards from the shoulder joints so that the wrists go through the vertical position to look rather like a classical oriental statue; we have arrived at the "Flip" (see Plate 2).

As the starting place in the arm balance is *Flop*, it is probably better to go to *Flop-flip* rather than the other way round. Do this *Flop-flip* exercise to a chosen pulsed tune to achieve the true natural feeling. Now pause in the *Flip* position and look at the left hand. If you have allowed the wrist to sit exactly where it wants to on the end of the forearm and not "positioned" by bending it backwards, you will have discovered the natural "giving hand" position (see Plate 22). We will return to this exercise when we deal with the right hand and bow and later with the left hand.

Posture

Finding "The Cradle"

The old and well tried physical exercise "hands on hips, up on your toes, knees bend, down on your haunches and up again in time to the music" will find us the balanced posture we are looking for. You will notice that when you do this exercise that in order to maintain perfect balance the knees bow outwards slightly, forming a natural cradle to accept the lower part of the 'cello. When you are in the lower position down on your haunches all that would be required to complete the ideal balanced posture is a chair of the required height to be placed underneath to take your weight off the leg muscles. As proof of this it is possible to play the 'cello for a short period without any support from a chair or stool, but the strain on the thigh muscles is too great to make this a practical exercise apart from demonstrating that it is the only position in which the whole body is in balance whilst playing the 'cello (Plates 3 & 4).

To avoid the feeling of immobility and being stuck to a chair we will have to call on the pulse for help once more.

Do the singing and clapping exercise with the knees flexing naturally, but this time lower yourself pulse by pulse on to the front edge of the chair that you have positioned carefully beforehand. Imagine that you have a large coiled spring or expandable shooting stick underneath you which gives and supports you with each pulse downwards. The most important part of the whole exercise is the moment you feel contact with the chair. This is the moment to bounce up again as though you have made contact with a cushion of air, otherwise you will lose the feeling of mobility and balance. The ideal is to feel the potential of being able to bounce up on the front of the chair on the pulse all the time you are playing, rather than being slumped in a fixed position.

The height of the chair is important. As no two people are exactly the same there can be no general rule for this, but if the thighs are parallel with the floor it would indicate that the seat is too low. This of course depends upon the size of the 'cello in relation to the person using it, but as a guide, the thighs should slope downward slightly from the hips to the knees.

As we always try to find out what happens and never "position" any part of our body, it is important to achieve the posture in balance naturally *and to know that we have done so.* You will notice that when you have achieved the naturally balanced posture the trunk will be slightly inclined forwards with the head and neck perfectly balanced on the shoulders. The lower part of the legs below the knees with the ankles and feet will be inclined backwards towards the chair legs, the heels inclined towards one another and the toes pointing outwards on the floor. The last small adjustment when you finally come in contact with the "cushion of air" (chair) is to allow the heels to rest gently on the floor. Because at the start of the exercise you have been up on your toes, if you are in posture with your heels still off the floor this would cause tension in the upper leg muscles (see Plates 3, 4, and 5).

We are now ready to have the 'cello presented to the balanced posture for which of course initially we will have to ask the help of another person (see Plates 4 and 5). Allow the top of the back of the 'cello to rest on the chest and the lower part of the instrument to be cradled by the naturally bowed part of the calves. Just as the arm balance allows the arms to swing gently, so it is possible for the "cradle" to be opened outwards and closed inwards gently by feeling the hips to be large oiled hinges swinging in balance. This will allow the knees and calves to swing away from the point of contact with the 'cello and swing gently back again to make the "Cradle".

Try to feel that this area of contact is full of air to avoid any tendency to grip with knees and calves. The lower part of the peg box will be some inches above the left shoulder and depending upon the size of the pegs the 'cello will be slightly inclined to the left to ensure that the head is not pushed out of balance to the right. At this stage the end pin is not extended as we want to find out what happens, when the 'cello is presented to the natural posture. Only when you feel that the 'cello is comfortably cradled is the end pin extended to the floor, which gives us the correct length of pin.

Ask your helper to take the 'cello away from you by taking hold of the neck and pulling it forward away from you. There should be no resistance to this movement at all and you should hardly be aware that there is a 'cello when you have it, or that there isn't one when it is taken away. When the 'cello is returned to your cradle ask your helper to hold the neck and gently move it from side to side. If you are in balance you will find that the whole of your body rocks gently with the 'cello and it feels to be part of you. This sideways connection is surprisingly strong considering how tenuous the forwards and backwards connection is. Think of this latter connection as your trunk and the 'cello being two playing cards balanced in an inverted V on a table top to ensure the contact at the apex is of the lightest (see Plate 5).

As we have achieved a balanced posture the next work is to ensure that we can maintain the feeling of mobility. We must consider the nature of the 'cello and our relationship to it. Like all members of the stringed instrument family it is beautifully designed and constructed, and like all living things, the better it is treated the better it will respond. We will be discussing our tactile relationship with the instrument throughout all our work, but for now we should discover how relatively light it is when in balance.

Stand up in front of a chair, with the left arm outstretched, holding the 'cello at the top of the neck just under the peg box. The 'cello should be resting on the floor with the endpin retracted; now lift the instrument off the floor with the outstretched left arm. After a few seconds you will have to lower it again due to arm-ache as you are feeling the full weight out of balance. Now sit down and place the 'cello across your knees and place the palm of either of your hands under the middle of the back of the 'cello, finding the balance point, and lift up the instrument on the palm of your hand, swinging it gently from side to side. You will notice immediately the difference between the weight out of balance and the weight in balance. The 'cello is comparatively light when in balance and when it swings gently from side to side it has an "alive" feeling.

We must now transfer this "alive" feeling of the 'cello to the balanced posture. For this we will have to use a melody in four pulses.

Example 1 a   "The Dancing Cello"

0   swing the cel-lo free, 0   swing it with-out care, 0   swing it so you real-ly feel the   cel-lo is-n't there.

Example 1 b (Schubert)

13

Take up the posture with the 'cello, endpin extended, resting in the cradle. Hold the crook of the neck, lightly, where it joins the body of the 'cello in the left hand, and on the first pulse, extend the left arm forwards in front of you. The 'cello is now vertical in front of you, resting on the endpin (Plate. 6a). On the second pulse swing the 'cello over to the right to be caught in the right hand (Plate 6b) and on the half pulse "and" release the left hand back to its first pulse position (Plate 6c) in order to receive the 'cello swinging back again on the third pulse (Plate 6d). The right hand and arm swing away again on the half pulse (Plate 6e). The fourth pulse flies the 'cello into the cradle again as the left arm finally closes (Plate 6f). Note that in Example 1a, the rhythm is 4-1-2-3 and NOT 1-2-3-4 as it is in the Schubert tune in Example 1b. This is the "Dancing 'Cello"

The purpose of this is to dispel any feeling that there may be that the 'cello is a large and heavy instrument, also to enhance the feeling of mobility, rather than being fixed behind the 'cello and firmly attached to the chair. Remember the feeling of bouncing up again when you first touch the chair in the posture exercise. This, along with the "dancing 'cello" exercise will produce the feeling that there is no 'cello as such.

In all our work on the mental and physical aspects of music making the concept that "there is no 'cello" and that "there is no bow" will play a major part. As the music comes from "inside-out" the instrument itself can be the prime cause of a blockage between our inner pulse song and our audience. That is why it is so important to organise the posture at the outset.

Plate 1: Suspended arms - "flop"

Plate 2: Suspended arms - "flip"

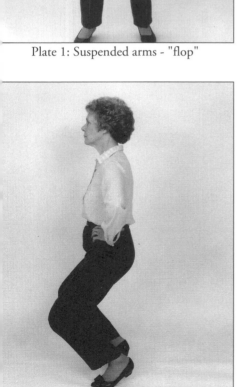

Plate 3: Hands on hips, knees bend "balance"
(mid position)

Plate 4: Mid position balance with 'cello

Plate 5: Final balanced position with 'cello and chair

Plate 6a: The dancing 'cello pulse four "o"
(see music example)

Plate 6d: Pulse two "cell"

Plate 6e: Pulse (two) <u>and</u> "lo"

Plate 6b: Pulse one "swing"

Plate 6c: Pulse (one) <u>and</u> "the"

Plate 6f: Pulse three "free"

Plate 7a: Suspended arms "flop"

Plate 7b: Higher to upper balance

Plate 7c: Lower to extended balance

Plate 9b: Bow connection "link and spread"

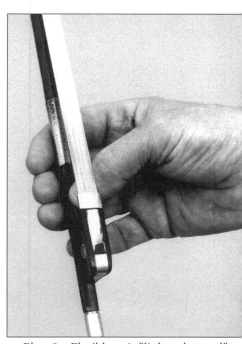

Plate 9c: Flexible unit "link and spread"

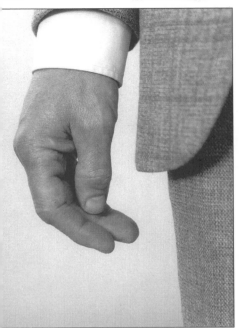

Plate 8: Preparing for bow connection

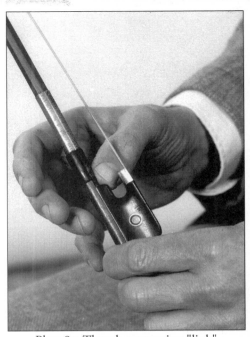

Plate 9a: Thumb connection "link"

Plate 10: Thumb "linked" with bow stick
and hair

Plate 11: "A bird in the hand"

Plate 12: Vertical bow balance feeling "the spread"

Plate 13: Middle by balance of the bow

Plate 15b: "Broken wing" - right arm out of balance

Plate 16: "The wing" - at the point of balanc

Plate 14: Middle by balance on the string

Plate 15a: "The wing"- right arm in balance

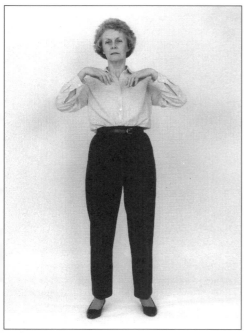

Plate 17a: The "swingswang". Initial "flop" position

Plate 17b: The "swingswang". Fully extended out-swing

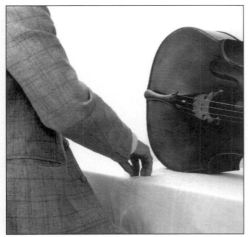

Plate 18a: Discovering the natural right arm movement

Plate 18b: Elbow opens

Plate 18e: Whole arm "concertinas" inward and returns to position as shown in plate 18a

Plate 19: Point of the bow. Right arm fully extended

Plate 18c: Fully extended

Plate 18d: Shoulder joint initiates movement backwards and behind

Plate 20: The "giving hand"

Plate 21: "sponging" the neck

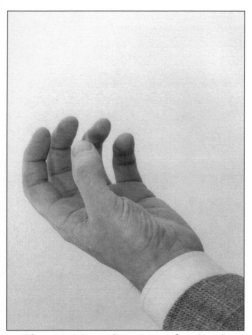

Plate 22: Minor disposition (fan closed)

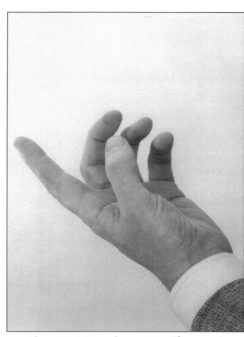

Plate 23: Major disposition (fan open)

Plate 26: First finger "sponges" into the string

Plate 27: "sponging" from behind into the third finger

Plate 24: The fan open, Major disposition

Plate 25: First finger curls into the string

Plate 28: The strength behind the fourth finger

Plate 29: "Skating" into the major disposition

Plate 30: Preparation for thumb position
(first part of Example 9)

Plate 31: Higher balance platform for thumb
(second part of Example 9)

Plate 32: Lower balance for thumb position
exercise

Plate 33: Shift to higher balance for thumb
position

Chapter 2

The Extended Balance
The Right Arm and Bow Connection

Take up the balanced posture with the 'cello and allow the arms to fall into the natural balance in the *flop* position (Plate 7a). Check that the lightest puff of wind could move the arms in their shoulder sockets, in fact it is always a good idea to use the power of the imagination in turning to each upper arm and blow lightly to achieve a swing response; *just a gentle movement!*

Place the index finger of the right hand, just as it falls naturally from the wrist, still in the *flop* position, on the left hand side of the G string and conversely the index finger of the left hand on the right hand side of the D string (Plate. 7b). Allow both arms to extend with the index fingers keeping contact with the strings until they reach the end of the fingerboard. The arms are now in the extended balance. (Plate 7c). Return to the normal balance by the opposite closing movement of the arms, always keeping the index fingers connected to the strings; this connection to the string with a slightly curved index finger will have great significance later. Make sure that you can see the backs of your hands which will ensure that both index fingers are tilting well backwards in relation to the string rather than being upright.

The object of this exercise is to transfer the feeling of having a weightless arm, or indeed no arm at all, in the normal high balanced state to that of the extended position where the right arm will produce the bow stroke. As far as the left hand is concerned you have just covered the whole range of movement required for almost all the positions on the 'cello, but of course we will be looking at the left hand in great detail in a later section.

Move from the normal balance to the extended state and back once or twice only, as over-repetition of an exercise tends to dull the focus of attention, thus destroying the freedom for which we search.

This is true of all the exercises we shall be doing. The key is to rest between each group of movements so that concentration of one's thoughts and feelings can be focused. Normally it is not possible to concentrate at the required level for more than a few moments at a time.

When you feel you have "no arms" in the extended balanced state, allow the left arm to hang by your side in order to concentrate on the right. For the time being you will have to store the feelings you have just experienced in your memory, as we shall have to find the connection with the bow and then return to the extended balance of the right arm before we discover the whole movement of the right arm.

Bow Connection

Allow the right arm to hang by your side, allowing the fingers and thumb slowly and gently to come into contact with each other (Plate 8). If things are working naturally you will find that the thumb and fingers are flexed and rounded. This is true of all our physical make-up in repose. If we look at anyone sitting in repose in a chair all the joints are flexed and curved; it would not be possible to be comfortable otherwise.

The point of contact between thumb and fingers would normally be between the tip of the thumb and the middle of the second finger. To be specific the middle of the second finger is the section between the end joint and the middle joint (the base joint being the third joint connecting the finger to the hand; the knuckle).

Without disturbing the finger-thumb connection, raise the arm up into the *flip* attitude so that you can see what has happened. With the left hand holding the nut of the bow, leaving the frog clear and the hair towards you, introduce the bow to the hand. Avoid the opposite movement of taking the hand to the bow as this tends to promote the feeling of grabbing.

At this stage the thumb is still lightly in contact with the finger. Aim the angle made by the front edge of the frog and the bow stick towards the tip of the thumb, and as it makes contact the stick will open the thumb-finger contact allowing the fingers to spread over the stick still partially curved (Plates 9a, 9b, and 9c). *The bow hair will contact the end section of the thumb just below the nail and, this contact will be with the full face of the thumb and though light, will be very strong. The thumb is the only digit which has this double contact with the stick and with the hair* (Plate. 10).

Notice that the fingers spread over the stick in a flexible unit but do not close too far in a grasping or grabbing attitude. The little finger rests near the top of the stick slightly flexed and very much at one with the rest of the fingers, but we will give the little finger a special look in the next exercise (Plate 11).

Release the left hand and with the bow connected in the right hand find the vertical balance of the bow. In fact the bow is not quite vertically balanced as it should be inserted into a right hand that has taken up the *flip* attitude (Plate 12). You will notice that the bow is inclined slightly away from you to the right and "the spread" of the four fingers feel the contact of the stick slightly more than if the bow had been truly vertical; this contact with the spread will be encountered a little later in the six points of the "connection". Visibly you will see almost all the hair with the stick hidden away behind it. In this position the bow should feel featherweight in the hand and if you ask a helper to remove the bow quickly from the hand sideways while your eyes are closed so you will not know when to expect its removal, the bow should come away without any resistance. On the other hand if you re-connect the bow and ask your helper to pull upwards from the bow tip you will find that, apart from the opening of the thumb from the fingers, there is no way that you could release the bow. *The bow connection is very strong without having to grip!* This is a very important point as this is the only way it is possible to connect the arm through the hand to the bow without gripping and thus being free from tension. Always feel that you are holding a soft ball, or even better, a small living bird in your hand which you don't want to harm (Plate 11). This rounding is felt in the whole hand including the palm, and is ever-present in everything we do with both hands. The lack of tension in this vital connection, along with the balanced use of the right arm driven on the pulse, is responsible for an uninhibited resonance on the open strings.

We should perhaps pause at this stage to consider the nature of sound. We will assume that you understand that a vibration, whether in a column of air or, as in this case, a string, consists not only of the fundamental note but a whole series of harmonics (otherwise called overtones or upper partials). The scientific explanation of the harmonic series can be found in most textbooks, so suffice it to say here that the quality of a sound is dependant on the natural harmonics or overtones contained in that sound. We will come back to the harmonic series again when we come to work on the left hand, and in the chapter on harmonics.

Example 2. Harmonic Series

If we apply pressure to vibrate the string we will choke out the possibility of generating overtones which will bring the sound alive. We must discover how to vibrate a string so that we can allow the vibration to generate the required number of overtones to produce a living sound. This is "sonority" and we are in the process of discovering how to produce it, first on the open strings by using the bow through the movements of the right arm in balance riding on the pulse, then later in conjunction with the left hand.

To be accurate, from a scientific point of view, it is not the *number* of overtones or harmonics that we are looking to increase but their amplitude in order to bring alive and make more active the overtones which are already there and which are always there in any sound to a greater or lesser degree.

The whole process is a constant search for the overtones to produce the true sonority which cannot be done with pressure. This does not mean that lack of pressure indicates weakness; on the contrary the forces we are channelling through the instrument are extremely powerful, just as water itself is not particularly strong but when channelled properly can move mountains!

As we have paused to look at the nature of sound it may be good idea also to look at the nature of our thumbs.

Medical experts tell us that the thumbs have a strong connection with a part of the brain which controls our tongue and consequently has a bearing on our speech. This being so, our thumbs must play a very important part in the process of communication. Look at the typical continental European gesticulating and you will see how the thumbs round into the fingers as his arms and hands move and wave to make his point.

Our thumbs are our most important digits. We could manage to pick up things and use our hands more or less normally without an odd finger or two, but without our thumbs we could do very little with our hands; this is why engineers often just insure their thumbs.

It is so important to allow our thumbs the freedom to transmit the power from the back muscles through the arm, hand and bow to the string. The most likely place in this chain to cause a blockage is in the thenar muscle, which is the large muscle at the base of the thumb where it joins the palm. This blockage, caused by anxiety, is manifested by the hand "grabbing" the bow.

To feel the extent of this problem, press hard with the thumb into the fingers opposite and with the fingers of the other hand feel how hard and rock-like the thenar muscle has become. Still pressing the thumb against the fingers cup the elbow in the other hand to feel how tense all the other muscles in the arm have become. Release the grip and feel how soft and spongy the thenar has become as well as all the other muscles in the arm.

The term "Bow grip" has a great deal to do with the problem

of forcing the life-giving blood out of the thumb muscle and stopping the power flow. This is just one example of how a generally accepted term by its very inference can be responsible for the tension we are trying to avoid.

The bow connection described above is the only way that the hand and bow can be connected without the use of pressure, so negating tension. It is of course possible to "grip" in the bow connection by applying pressure, but it is not necessary to apply pressure to remain in connection. With any other bow hold it needs counter-pressure with the stick between the thumb and fingers in order to hold it.

As we said in the Introduction, this bow connection is perhaps the main reason why a great number of 'cellists cannot wholly accept the "New Approach" mainly on the grounds that it has not been done before. Surely if it is a fundamental principle that works on the violin it must also work on the 'cello? Did not someone say that if the great J. L. Duport were to return he would surely expect to find that the technique of the 'cello had progressed and developed beyond the stage at which he had left it? In Duport's "Essay" on 'cello playing there is a very interesting comment regarding contact with the bow hair. He said that as the hair was in contact with the string he liked to be in contact with the hair. This was achieved by allowing the long second finger to overlap the stick until it touched the hair on the opposite side to the thumb.

The great 'cellist Casals from time to time suffered cramp in the large thenar muscle of the right hand which indicated physical tension through having to grip the bow. However, he no doubt was able to compensate for this problem higher up the arm. So how much more do we need to help ourselves by discovering ways of avoiding this kind of tension?

How much better then to have one of our prime articulators in direct contact with the hair and stick, and also to ensure that there is a positive release of tension. This writer found the concept of the bow connection very exciting as the Hungarian 'cellist, Vilmos Palotai, with whom he studied before coming into contact with the "New Approach" used a bow hold which was almost "the connection". It just needed the *slightest* rotation into the thumb and there it was!

Another objection to the thumb connection is that it tends to angle the bow stick "away" rather than "to" the player, which may be so, but surely that is of no importance if we achieve the sonority for which we are searching! In fact, if the true feeling is discovered the full flat of the hair will be presented to the string. An interesting experiment has been tried many times where a 'cellist will ask a group of listeners to say which sound they prefer, one with the thumb connected and the other without the connection. They always choose the one with the connection because they are aware that a blockage has been removed and there is a consequent increase in the amplitude of the overtones which enhance the quality.

The crux of this problem lies in the fact that there must be a general feeling of "roundness" and "softness" in the right hand, which was Palotai's approach; the thumb "connection" is just a development of this feeling needing the minutest adjustment rounding into the thumb. In this case particularly, and in all cases of true learning, *it is better to look for the spirit of the law rather than observe the letter of the law.*

We will approach the bow connection from another angle now, but before we do, make sure that you have the true feeling of the connection with the bow in the *flip* balanced position, checking that the thenar muscle is soft and spongy and that "there is no bow".

Take up the posture with the 'cello, and find the middle by balance of the bow by balancing it on the back of the index finger (Plate 13). The left hand can now place the bow on either the D or G string at the point of balance (Plate 14). With the left hand still holding the bow in place with the stick but well clear of the frog, open the thumb of the right hand from the fingers a little to perform a "docking manoeuvre" with the thumb into the connection already described as in Plate 10. This is the first of six actions called *link.* The second is to allow the fingers to fall naturally over the stick in a sort of soft naturally rounded unit, making sure not to over-round the fingertips into a grab (Plates 9c and 11). This is *spread.* Because the little finger usually wants to take on the whole weight of the bow in front of it, a very unfair contest, we should make sure that the little finger is rounded just touching the top of the stick and just giving it a little flex; this is *curl.* Now we can take away the left hand and as the bow is in balance resting on the string we should feel the same connection with the bow that we felt in the vertical position (Plate 15a).

The next feeling is to make sure all the joints, shoulder, elbow and wrist are free to move as in a bath of oil. Allow the whole to flex a little. This is *give.* As a preparation to the bow stroke imagine the right arm to be in the weightless condition which the whole arm balance will give us. This will allow us to feel the potential movement of the bow stroke. This is *fly.*

The last of the six is *smile,* which might sound strange, but it ensures that as we have been concentrating hard on establishing all parts of the connection, we do not cause tensions in other parts of the body and that we cultivate a feeling of general well-being. This last point is true of all the actions we learn!

Chapter 3

The Bow Stroke

The shape of the bow-stick itself gives us a clue as to how the stroke will work naturally. The curve starts its downward course gradually until about two-thirds of its length and then climbs comparatively steeply to the point. When all the preliminary actions leading up to the full bow stroke are completed, we shall see that the natural arm movement will describe this shape.

Firstly we must find the true middle of the bow, which is the middle by balance not the middle by measurement, as we did in the previous chapter to find the connection.

Extend the index finger of the left hand and place the bow sideways across it, i.e. the stick and the edge of the hair touching the finger, to find the spot where the bow balances horizontally which will be approximately a third of its measured length from the nut. This is the *middle by balance*. (see Plate 13)

After taking up the posture with the 'cello, place the bow at the point of balance on the G string with the left hand (see Plate 14). Allow the right arm to take up the arm balance in the *flop* position, curling the index finger into the G string to run down towards the bow to find the extended balance. Without losing the feeling of the extended balance leave the contact of the G string with the index finger to "dock" the thumb into the *link* which is the first part of the connection exercise. Continue the connection with *spread, curl, give, fly* and *smile*.

You will now specifically feel the *give* in the whole arm and the potential of the *fly* if the arm is still in balance. Also the bow hair will feel to be glued to the G string through the connection. The slight movement in the *give* and the *fly* section will give you the feeling for the G string level. The feeling for the level will be reproduced on each string and can be most easily sensed by the **outside edge of the upper arm**. Imagine that a mercury balance runs along this back edge of the upper arm and has four points corresponding to the level of each string. With a natural rotation of the whole arm initiated by the shoulder joint, balance the bow in the vertical position (see Plate 12). This movement is not just an arm rotation on the spot but includes a small, gracious sideways movement taking the lower arm and hand away from the body via a slight opening of the elbow joint, remembering that it is initiated from the shoulder joint.

Conversely, when returning into the G string again, the movement contains this sideways component as well as rotation. We will return to this again shortly when we discuss "Hovering".

The eyes can play a very useful part in this exercise. When the bow is in the vertical position look at the point on the G string where the area of the outside of the upper arm will eventually guide the hair. Try to think of the four strings and fingerboard as a single inclined unit into which you are going to dock the bow hair at the four slightly different levels. It is usually the stick which comes to mind first when we are looking at the bow, but it is the hair which does the work, the stick merely holds the hair. As the bow comes into the string finding its true level, transfer the eyes to the upper arm to see it actually controlling the whole arm to find the required level. Say aloud "G" with each action, repeating the exercise on each string, remembering to give yourself the named command each time. The eyes are working on the upper arm almost like a magnetic force helping it to find its balance for the string you have asked it to find.

Notice how the connection responds when the bow comes into the string from the vertical position. If everything is in balance the connection will always be rounded and soft with the "bird in the hand" feeling very much in evidence. As the whole movement is a co-ordinated balanced action the connection always remains the same and is unaffected and when the bow hair is resting "glued" to the string; it is the string that takes the balanced weight of the bow.

Notice the level of the arm in Plates 15a and 15b and how it feels like a bird's wing with the fingers like the tip feathers. This could be called the "bird's wing" attitude. However, if the upper arm is too low and the mercury balance is lost, the result is as in Plate 15b where the bird's wing feeling is also completely lost.

Now the obvious question is "What happens to the little finger when I hold the bow above the string?" The short answer is that you never hold the bow hovering above the string! Perhaps this answer would not satisfy a more advanced player at this stage but have patience as we shall test the validity of this as we expand on the bow stroke.

The question itself comes about by moving the bow from the balanced vertical position to the horizontal in mid-air without an instrument. This should never happen in practice, but if it does it will cripple the little finger as it asked the impossible task of taking the whole bow weight, like a lever in front of it; just compare the length and weight of the bow stick with that of the little finger and see how unfair is the contest!

We have now arrived at the position of having the right arm and hand in balance in connection with the bow resting on the G string at the point of balance. Check through the six points of the connection exercise again giving particular attention to *curl* just in case the little finger is tempted to do any holding! (see Plate 16)

Ask a helper to give a very small gentle pull on the inside middle of the upper arm and release immediately. If you have set up the connection correctly and imagined the *fly* part well, the result should be *two* quaver G's (Pa-Pa or G-G). As only one small action has been initiated by your helper you are getting "two for the price of one" because your arm swings back on a muscular reflex naturally to regain its original position. It must be stressed that we are talking about very small movements here, and the kind of quaver movement will not just depend on the movement, made later by yourself, but on the inner energy you send through to command the arm movement. Initiate the movement yourself now by *first* feeling the inner quaver pulse giving yourself the command "G-G" aloud, then motivate the arm from the shoulder joint to describe small shallow arcs near the point of balance where the hair is in contact with the string. Out comes two G's. Then try G-G-G-G four quavers and so on until you can go on producing quavers indefinitely. It must be stressed that however many quavers you wish to play you must give yourself the aural command first. If you require two groups of four quavers say G-G-G-G / G-G-G-G, or if six, as in compound time, GGG / GGG. You will soon feel the natural difference between the simple and the compound pulses, the former will work with the down or up direction coming relatively in the same place in each group, whereas in the latter (compound time) the down and up direction of the bow alternates, i.e. down - up - down: up - down - up. It must be said that all the smaller divisions of the quaver or quicker quaver movement are produced in exactly the same way but with a comparatively quicker but smaller movement.

As we have said, all the movement is initiated by the strong back and shoulder muscle activating the shoulder joint which produces the small shallow swinging arcs. *The elbow and wrist joints are flexible parts of the whole movement but do not initiate any movement of their own.* If they do, the whole movement will lose power and control with the strong inner pulse not being able to be transmitted through to the string.

Those of you who are interested in things mechanical will understand the function of a heavy flywheel or a governor in a piece of machinery. Both these devices provide control to the movement of the whole. The governor prevents ungoverned spasmodic movements from the power source, such as a clockwork spring, reaching the last moving parts in the mechanical chain so that the clock will tick once every second.

Although this is a mechanical analogy the forces of which we speak are universal and spring from nature and are in no way mechanical in the narrow sense we have been using the term to describe "outside-in".

So it is *balanced* movement which produces control, and our balanced movement in the right arm comes from the large shoulder muscle operating the shoulder joint, all other joints are follow-through movements activated by the big joint, which is our flywheel. The working of the smaller elbow or wrist joint, if activated by these joints, is analogous to the spasmodic and ungoverned uncoiling of the mainspring in a clockwork motor.

It would be a good idea to have a look at the staccato quaver at this stage because the moderately moving quaver appears more than any other kind for the 'cellist in accompanying passages and is called thrown spiccato. It is sometimes referred to as "off the string", and it is the idea behind this phrase which is responsible for crippled little fingers, as the term implies we hold the bow off the string to do this and the little finger pays the price!

As we shall see, all movements in the right shoulder and arm are organised in balance throughout the whole bow stroke. Any small segment of this stroke, as this quaver movement, works in exactly the same way for the short distance it travels as it does for that same section in the full bow stroke.

So to discover the staccato quaver movement set the legato quavers going for four G's (or D's) and continue for another four but this time imagine the large back and shoulder muscle is a winch which winches up the whole arm very slightly, just allowing the lower part of the arcs you are describing to brush the string; the whole arm, bow and hair absorb any shock, and the result will be clearly articulated bell-like sounds produced by exactly the same movements as in the legato quavers. Check the *curl* in the little finger and you will find that because of the swinging movement in balance there is no need to hang on with the little finger.

Now that we have made contact with the string and experienced some movements, albeit small ones, we must go straight into the full bow stroke. The movement required by the right arm to produce the full bow stroke is something we probably do many times a day without giving it a thought.

Stand up and find the arm balance in the *flop* position, and then send the arms out forwards in front of you, and return to the balance again. Just swing out and up, and swing back and down, as always to a pulse. Always allow the wrists and fingers to hang naturally, allowing them to go where they want to in a "follow-through" action. This is the *swingswang* (Plates 17a and 17b). Note that there is no pause between the *swing* and the *swang*, i.e. the *swang* is a natural and immediate response to the *swing*, therefore *swingswang*. Place your 'cello, resting on its side, in front of you on a table of normal height, such as a dining or kitchen table. Sit on a chair opposite the lower and wider part of the instrument facing the tailpiece, stretch out the right hand to see if you can easily reach the rib just before it curves down to where it joins the neck (Plates. 18 a - f). Take a small coin between finger and thumb of the right hand and adopt the arm balance in the *flop* position with both arms, now with the right arm alone, keeping the palm of the hand always facing the floor, reach out and place the coin on top of the rib and return to the balance, go out again, pick up the coin and return to the balance.

Let us find out what is happening in these movements. In the movement out the arm joints open, initiated by the large shoulder joint and followed very soon by the elbow joint opening as well. From the arm balance position of the right arm, cup the right elbow in the palm of the left hand and push gently with the left hand on the point of the elbow joint. This push should initiate the opening of the elbow joint, having a bearing on the shoulder hinge and wrist.

Notice that this action is exactly the same movement as previously described in the *swingswang*, but highlights the function of the elbow opening and its relation to the other joints in the full *swing*. Another significant movement takes place at the end as we do the *swingswang* exercise; there is a small curved movement upwards towards the final opening out at a slightly steeper rate than the rest of the movement. Remember how we said at the beginning of the chapter that the shape of the bow stick was significant, so we see now that this arm movement describes this shape in front of us. Naturally let us see what happens in the opposite direction back to the balanced *flop* position. The first movement is a slight curve downwards which is initiated by the slight behind opening of the shoulder joint which in turn initiates the closing of the elbow joint (Plate 18d) and then the follow-through will be a collapse inwards of the joints together, with the big shoulder joint continuing the behind (rearward) movement. The inward movement is exactly the reciprocal of the outward movement. The part that needs a careful look is the movement which initiates the inward move. Although the elbow joint closes first, it is working in conjunction with the big shoulder joint which opens and moves backwards to keep the whole movement in line. An error, which would break the natural movement, is to flex the elbow joint alone without the co-ordinated backward movement of the shoulder joint.

The first *swingswang* exercise gives us the bow arm movement in front of us. The second exercise where we place a coin on the rib of the 'cello gives us the movement in the same direction we shall use the full bow stroke (Plate 18). It should be a similar feeling to opening and closing a door.

It should be stressed that the full bow stroke is an easy and natural swing and once achieved is as natural and automatic as breathing. We could try to analyse the process by finding out what each muscle does, what each joint does and would probably finish by writing a whole volume on the subject which would defeat the object, which is to convince oneself that "there is no bow", just an easy swing on the pulse. It would be much better if we could overturn convention and call a down bow an *outward* bow and an up bow an *inward* bow.

With this in mind, find the level in balance at the heel of the bow in exactly the same way that we found the string at the point of balance but this time as near to the heel as possible. As a start choose either of the middle two strings, G or D. Choose a pulse that will be somewhere near a second, i.e. 60 crotchets to the minute, and with the full bow movement we have just discovered *swing* to the point and *swang* to the heel. The term *swingswang* is coined from *swang* being the reciprocal of *swing* or to turn the Newtonian physics upside down, "what goes down must come up". So *swingswang* is the complete natural whole bow action down and up (or outwards and inwards).

Always remember to give yourself the appropriate pulse command, (e. g. D-D), before making the movement, and when you do, "magnetise" the upper arm with your eyes saying inwardly "swingswang". Your eyes will check that the arm is doing what it was doing in the pre-bow exercises with the coin on the 'cello rib (Plate 18).

If everything is working correctly on all four strings there is literally nothing more to learn about the right arm and bow because all smaller divisions of the full bow swing can be isolated in the particular segment required and the true movement discovered from its position in the full swing. However, it is rare to find that everything falls into place at once, so it is a good idea first of all to divide up the full bow swing and look at the movements more closely; we shall also find how the bow swing is naturally part of the flow of music.

Before doing this we should look again at the levels of the various strings in the context of the full bow swing. Remember the mercury balance on the outer edge of the upper arm which guides the whole arm to the required level? When you are changing from the D string level in the *swingswang* exercise up to the A string (after pausing two pulses!), notice how little the upper arm needs to be raised to find the A string level. It is a common problem to over-react to the A string level and imagine that you have to climb a mountain with the upper arm to reach the required level; just another hot-bed of tension! Also notice that in crossing from the G string to the C string the right arm seems to be further behind you and folded more than you might have imagined. The problem here is that the upper arm does not fold enough behind at the heel, which causes a distorted wrist joint and again the inevitable tension. The shoulder hinge, elbow, wrist and connection is a flexible unit which, by adjustment at the shoulder joint, remains *relatively* the same at all times and on whatever string in whatever segment of the whole bow swing it may be.

Notice how the wrist is flexed at the heel as in the *flop* balance position, and how it "gives" towards the point as the other joints open out. Also the connection in the hand remains basically the same but is *never* rigid and accommodates the required adjustment during the down and up bow. The most important fact to remember is that the motivation comes from the big shoulder joint, triggered by the inner pulse; all the other joints react as a follow-through to produce the natural swing.

We will now divide the full bow swing into two parts. You will already have a good understanding of the middle by balance as we did the eighth notes, quavers, there. Find the balance at the heel again on a middle string and give yourself two quarter notes, crotchet, pulses (1:2) and swing the arm from the shoulder joint from the heel to the middle by balance on these pulses. Now rest, still keeping the balance and the *fly* feeling and say "pause-pause" on the pulse. On the third and fourth pulses swing out to the point (Plates 15a, 16 and 19).

The reason for dividing the full bow swing like this is to find out what is happening. You will notice that the upper arm is driven from the shoulder joint for the first part of the operation and after the pauses the elbow hinge begins to open when you leave the middle by balance until it is fully open at the point; it depends on physical characteristics how much the elbow hinge has to open. Long-armed tall people will not be fully open at the point, whereas short-armed short people may not be able quite to make the point fully opened. This is not important because we are only talking of a very small length of bow which probably cannot be used. So for the short-armed people it is better to be free from tension than to try to eke out the last fraction of the bow. The long-armed people have their problems too, such as having to fold up considerably more on the C string to maintain the true balance and swing.

We left the movement suspended at the point of the bow waiting for the up bow swing. Before we do this we will have to find the "mirror" image of the middle by balance. This is simply a point on the bow which is the same distance from the point as the middle by balance is from the heel. So after "pause-pause" at the point of the bow, pulses 1 and 2 will be initiated by a fold of the arm made by the shoulder joint moving the upper arm slightly opening back-wards co-ordinated with the elbow hinge closing. It is of great importance to understand this particular movement because if the elbow hinge closes without the help of the upper arm through the shoulder joint, an ugly bow "push" will result at the start of the up bow.

Now pulse 1 : 2 with this movement we have discovered to the mirror balance point, say "pause-pause" then the pulses 3 : 4 will be the large closing to the heel. Again the main movement is started by the elbow hinge, always in co-ordination with the shoulder joint, and towards the middle by balance the opposite becomes true; less elbow hinge and nearly all shoulder.

Say "pause-pause" at the heel and then repeat the operation only two or three times, never allowing the exercise to become unmusical or mechanical. The next stage is to leave out the pauses, pulsing four on the down swing and the same on the up swing noticing how the change at the heel, and particularly at the point, swings through naturally. If the bow change becomes self-conscious it will cause all sorts of unwanted accents but if it is part of a natural swing it will always be part of the music. The end of the down bow is like the Indian rope trick, it could stay suspended for as long or as little as required and it will be seen later in the left hand section how valuable this feeling will be.

Although even a simple analysis of the full bow swing takes a large number of words and ideas to explain, the action itself is completely free and natural; circus artists do similar actions and much more complicated ones without a conscious thought, so our work is to discover how to enjoy the feeling of having no bow, just an easy swing.

You will notice that the greater amount of movement in the arm in both directions of the bow occurs in the second part. In other words, there is a natural acceleration from the beginning to the end of each swing.

If we were to divide the bow into equal measured parts we should get equally measured beats which go nowhere. Is not the nature of music a flow from somewhere to somewhere else? So with the natural swing of the right arm we have just discovered, do we not serve music exactly? The swing always produces a feeling of anticipation; that it is growing and going somewhere, whereas moving to the middle by measurement in two pulses, and the same to the point in two more is essentially a static experience.

The three-pulse bow swing underlines the situation even more strongly. Pulses one and two go to the middle by balance, pulse three alone goes all the way to the point in the down bow. In the up bow pulses one and two go to the mirror point of balance and three alone goes all the way back to the heel as the whole arm folds inwards in a co-ordinated swing.

We will deal with the different types of bowing in greater detail when we have dealt with the left hand, for reasons that will be obvious then, but we could perhaps look at one particular type now as it deals with a rather neglected area, that being the upper section from the mirror point of balance to the point and back.

The Détaché and the Martelé are terms which are perhaps not always understood. Specifically the Détaché is the legato form of the Martelé, so by discovering the Détaché first, the Martelé will follow naturally.

The détaché is the legato swing from the mirror point of balance to the point on the down bow and the other way on the up bow. There is no exact "tape measure" restriction over this because if the tempo desired is quick the swing will be shorter and if slower the swing will be greater, thus overshooting the mirror point of balance. The movement is exactly that of the whole bow stroke in this particular section. Do just two strokes *swingswang* and pause. You will feel the governor or flywheel control very strongly from the shoulder hinge with the follow-through of the rest of the arm. It is in fact the elbow hinge which is doing the opening and closing in this movement but it is *always* initiated by the shoulder joint.

As with all other right arm work search for the sonority, that is the overtones in the string you are vibrating. This is particularly so in the détaché and martelé as the tendency is to misjudge the speed of movement and produce a "skidding bump" instead of a clear sonority. Think of the legato détaché stroke at about crotchet equals 60 at first and only increase speed when you have discovered the sonority. The martelé is exactly the same, except it is a staccato note. At first try it as a ($♪$ ⌐) and later if a greater degree of staccato is required try it as ($♪$ ⌐ ⌐).

Example 3

Détaché (quaver pulses)   Martelé

1 2 3 4 5 6 7 8   1 2 3 4 5 6 7 8

33

Try the détaché legato in crotchets, but pulsing in eight quavers, that is 1:2, 3:4, 5:6, 7:8 (quaver = 120). For the four crotchets in a bar the martelé will be done by the swing on the odd number pulses and pauses on the even number pulses. It is even more important not to allow the swing to over-react in the martelé as the "skidding bumps" will certainly take over. The quality to be sought is a bell-like sound where the maximum amount of overtones are produced at the start of the swing and are allowed to decay naturally. We can organise specific work for the détaché and martelé when we come to the left hand.

The détaché and martelé highlight the change of bow at the point, the movements for which we discussed in the full bow swing. Changes of bow at the heel are done with the same movements that we discovered in the quavers, that is the swing back or "nudge" done by the shoulder hinge. If the swing is working correctly the change of bow will take care of itself, because each change is part of the natural swing back and needs no separate work of its own. In fact by trying consciously to produce a smooth change of bow, more often than not we fuss and fret over the problem and produce exactly the opposite of that which we most desire and obtain an unwanted accent for our pains!

The overall function of the right arm is the basic sound generator, just as is the breath for a singer and wind player or the mechanical / electrical box of tricks which produces the wind in an organ. In each case it is some other factor which is responsible for making the music from that sound generator such as the fingers through the organ keys or the control of the vocal chords in the voice.

There is one question which is often asked. "Whereabouts do I use the bow between the bridge and fingerboard to produce the best sonority?" Obviously there is no fixed answer to that; it depends on the sonority required, Mozart's sonority will generally not be Bartok's sonority and there will be all sorts of variation in quality even within the same composition. The general answer is that the whole arm responds to the type of sonority required. If you touch a snail with a stick it will quickly retreat into its shell. If the right

34

arm is producing too bright or harsh sonority it will fold a little bringing it into the softer region nearer the fingerboard. This is an instinctive reaction to the requirements of the music.

When we are convinced that "there is no bow," only free natural movement producing the sonority we want through the pulse, we can move on to our music maker which is, of course, the left hand.

Chapter 4

The Left Hand - The Music Maker

We come now to the heart of conscious music making which is manifest through the left hand. As we have said, the two main ingredients without which music, of the kind with which we are here involved, cannot exist, are pulse and interval. Pulse is all-pervasive through every action we make, but we can only produce four notes, making intervals of fifths on the open strings, without the use of the left hand.

We shall discover that the left hand is the music maker. Through the movement of the knuckles of the left hand we shall learn to shape and sculpt the intervals.

It is an important concept to realise that we do not deal with individual notes, as a note in isolation has no normal musical meaning. It is only when one note is related to another that we can have a musical experience. Kató Havas said that it is not the notes themselves that matter, it is what goes on between them that is important. Our work now is to discover what is the function of the left arm and hand, to find the "glue" between the notes and mould them into the musical intervals.

Take up the balanced posture with the 'cello, the arms in balance in the *flop* position. Swing into the *flip* position, focusing your attention on the left arm and hand then allow your right arm to hang by your side out of the way. If you have gone to the *flip* position naturally the left hand will sit on top of the forearm in what can be described as the "giving hand" position. This means that the hand is neither positioned by the wrist forwards nor backwards on the arm but just sits comfortably where it wants to be, held by the natural springiness of muscles and tendons (Plate 20). You will notice that in the *flop* position the hands and fingers hang downwards to the floor but as the arm swings upwards through the vertical you will feel this springiness in the wrist preventing the hand from falling over too far in the opposite direction and the fingers will want to close a little as though holding a sponge.

Go through this action a few times always noticing what is happening. When you are sure you have experienced the giving hand position you are ready to make contact with the neck and fingerboard with the left hand.

From the giving hand position, allow the left arm to move inwards, always in balance, towards the neck of the 'cello. This movement is analogous to the movement of the right arm when it moves from the vertical bow position into the chosen string. It is a sideways concertina-like movement allowing the hand to close round the neck as though it was getting hold of a sponge, the whole hand being rounded, including the palm; this feeling is ever-present in everything we do with the left hand (Plate 21).

It is important to realise that this is in no way the movement back to the *flop* position in which the elbow is raised and the wrist, as the arm goes through the vertical, allows the hand to drop, thus arching the wrist in the natural *flop*. If we transfer the *flop* position directly to the neck we will have an arched wrist which will in turn produce tensions in the arm and wrist as soon as we try to use the knuckles and fingers in a playing context. It is obvious that the natural springiness in the wrist when it is in the "giving hand" position is what we are looking for when we come to use the left hand on the instrument.

The main object of this first exercise is to ensure that the hand and wrist should not be "positioned" but extend naturally out of the forearm having a slight concave look viewing it from the back of the hand. Conversely, if this concave aspect is allowed to go too far (i.e. positioned) then you would stand a better chance of using the left hand, albeit under tension, with the wrist "flopped" in the arched position. However, let us find out what happens naturally and pursue the "giving hand".

When the fingers and thumb close round the neck imagine that the neck is made of soft spongy material rather than hard wood. This tactile awareness is of the utmost importance in order to prepare the left hand for its work in producing the sonority for which we are searching. How can we train the left hand towards the desired contact?

Take the hand away from the 'cello neck and place it round the front of your own neck as far as it will go and try to sing or talk with the same amount of contact that you had on the 'cello. Most likely you will find that you are throttling your song or speech, so release the contact until you can deliver freely and this will give you the idea of the contact you need with the 'cello neck.

Resuming the contact with the 'cello neck, allow the elbow to rise and fall gently, motivated by the big shoulder joint to discover the new lower balance of the whole arm. Allow the elbow to open out slightly so that the hand sponging the neck moves up the neck and fingerboard towards the ribs. This movement is of course downwards towards the floor and is the same movement we did earlier to find the extended balance.

Try to feel that the hand and wrist always maintains the same aspect to the neck, that is with a slight tilt backwards towards the first finger produced by the natural pronation in the balance. You will notice that if you straighten the wrists in the *flop* attitude the backs of the hands are very slightly tilted towards your body. As we move up the neck we must try to avoid the tendency which allows the forearm to rotate forwards towards the fourth finger as the elbow opens out. We will see later that this forward rotation is death to a free left hand, so make sure that the hand maintains the backward tilt wherever it finds itself. A few minutes each day of the sponging exercise will convince us that the 'cello neck, fingerboard and strings are indeed soft and spongy. **This is a caress not an exercise!**

Now with a slight movement of the left arm backwards and behind, initiated by the shoulder joint, which moves the elbow slightly more behind, the thumb and fingers will be drawn out of the closed sponge position so that the fingers will be in contact with the C string, and the thumb will be underneath the neck.

Just a little more movement away with the elbow dropping a fraction and we have the left hand in contact with the G string and so on to the D and A strings. This level searching is just the same as we found for the right arm but here the movements are so slight they are hardly noticeable. We will talk later about the concept of one large string rather than four separate ones when we come to interval shapes.

You will notice that as you allow the fingers to be drawn across the fingerboard from the C string to the A string with the left hand in the rounded sponged attitude, the finger ends first feel the side of the string nearest to you, or to be more specific, as someone in a workshop once observed, the "north-east" side of the string, meaning that if we take a *cross section* of a string making it a compass rose, north would be upwards away from the fingerboard, south downwards to the fingerboard, west sideways away from you to the left and east towards you to the right

We shall see that the finger contact somewhere between north and east on the string will be of great significance in the use of the left hand, and in the higher positions the contact will be slightly "easterly" and more rounded. Sponge the north-east side of the G string just allowing the fingers to make gentle contact, with the thumb gently resting underneath the neck. Allow the left arm to swing away (Plate 22) into the giving hand position (Plate 20) and look at the hand. Now imagine the fingers are vanes of a closed fan which you will now open. Notice how the first finger opens out away from you and the little finger comes towards you (Plate 23). Also notice what a great distance there is between the first and fourth fingers. If you place your left hand, palm down, on a flat table fanning it out as much as possible there would not be nearly the same distance between first and fourth fingers as in the previous case going through three dimensions. This is why physical stretching on any stringed instrument is not only undesirable but unnecessary!

Returning to the G string with the sponged hand but now still in contact, fan out the fingers as you did in the giving hand position. Actually the only thing to make any significant movement is the first finger which opens out towards the scroll, the thumb and top three fingers (i.e. the second, third and fourth) remaining more or less where they were (see Plate 24). Close the fan allowing the first finger to close again into the sponge.

Repeat this action, but this time allow the fingers to remain clear of the string, only allowing the first finger to make contact as it comes into the sponged position after fanning (Plates 25 and 26). The thumb is always in contact gently stroking the underside of the neck.

You will notice that as the first finger closes into the string, from behind forwards making contact on its back edge with the north-east side of the string, the other fingers sponge naturally towards it closing a little. The fourth finger will be quite high above the string and when we come to use the other fingers they will spring out again quite naturally. The watchword is "mobility" as the left hand is always "alive". We will amplify this idea later.

What we have done so far is to guide the left hand into shaping the first interval, that of a tone or whole step, between the open string and the first finger. The word "step" is useful to us in gaining a better understanding of the interval shaping process. Even better, think of a skater making the initial movement to start skating. There must be a swing from the hips (the big joints again!) from behind forwards, to set the whole body in motion and from then on one swing motivates the next combining into an integrated whole. Each couple of movements is analogous to an interval on the fingerboard. Do you think the skater is aware of the skates? No, the awareness is of the whole movement with the skates as an extension of the body making contact with the ice. This is analogous to the shaping of the intervals; we skate into the string with the first finger to produce a sculpted interval. We could easily produce notes in the way a mechanical robot walks in jerky unco-ordinated steps. This is what happens when we bang fingers down on top of the string.

So far we have only been making movements without producing sounds with the left hand in an approximate area of the fingerboard and neck. Now we will have to discover how to find the note A on the G string.

Perhaps to start with, it would be better to do it pizzicato, a facet of string playing often overlooked. But at present suffice it to say that the right arm in balance is brought into the upper part of the fingerboard with the thumb contacting the C string edge of the fingerboard with the fingers rounded above the G string. Round the fleshy tip of the first finger (or second if preferred) into the western side of the G string to pluck the note G. This is a balanced movement in which the whole arm takes part but it is the knuckle joint of the right hand which produces the articulation, which as we have seen, is exactly the same as with the left hand. This should produce a clear bell-like quality on the open string. (See later chapter on Pizzicato).

Of all that has gone before and all that is to come, this next section is the key to it all; without it nothing else is of any significance.

After you have heard the open G string, *sing* G and then *sing* A. Or if you prefer sing Do then Re. Now with the first finger action of the left hand we have just discovered, come into the G string and find the tone interval (see Plates 24, 25 and 26). You can check the A with the first finger by plucking the open A string an octave above. When you are happy with this feeling sing G-A; A-G, then pluck the intervals as the left hand sculpts open-first; first-open, always on a singing pulse.

Now on to the next interval using the major scale first, A to B, always sing the interval on the pulse first, then, after finding the A sonority, allow the second and third fingers to swing out coming from behind forwards to search for the B with the third finger. Notice how the thumb responds. It comes slightly forward and more underneath towards the active finger and always the third finger is searching for the north-east side of the string (never pressing down on top). As this happens the first finger is naturally released and opens out behind, just as in the analogy of the skater. As one skate is thrust forward the other swings backwards (from the hips) ready for the next swing. So we swing each finger through our knuckles from behind forwards and the interesting thing is that even on a descending interval, B to A, the first finger is fanned out to prepare the swing in, forwards from behind, to produce the A for the second time (Plate 27).

Now to the last interval on the G string which is the half-tone B to C. Sing B-C; C-B. If the movement is felt naturally on the fan the first finger will open out fully as the fourth finger swings in from the third to find C and the thumb will respond and move slightly forwards underneath again (Plate 28). If there is anything forced or positioned about this you will know that you have not discovered the natural movements for which we are searching. It is often said that our fourth, or little finger, is weak and therefore needs strengthening! Such ideas can lead to physical and mental damage. If you discover the feelings just described regarding the interval B to C you will have all the power you will ever need in the little finger because the powerhouse is much further back in the big shoulder joint.

When you are happy with the left hand so far, we can repeat all we have done with the right arm and bow instead of pizzicato. Because pizzicato is such a comparatively transient experience compared with the sustained bow we should pause to discuss sonority again. As we have discovered with our work on the right arm and bow, the quality of the sonority is controlled by the overtones or harmonics contained in the sound produced (see Harmonic Series, example 2). Now the left hand will have to make its contribution in producing the sonority.

Music depends for its existence on two main factors, movement and air, as do most living things. Rigidity and lack of air is death to music. But how often are we exhorted to press down on top of the string? The very words "stop the note" produce an idea contrary to the production of overtones which makes the sound alive. The very idea of vibrato is so often to make better a sound that is wanting. It is wanting because we are squashing and squeezing the life out of the sound and then trying to make it better by shaking a dead thing! It will be seen later that a true vibrato enhances the overtones and it does this as the outcome of a natural search; it is the overtones themselves that generate the vibrato.

If we first sing G-A and then swing from open string to first finger using the bow we will discover the overtones in A. The A can be enriched by rounding and sponging the left hand with the first finger softening, always rounded. The thumb and first finger make a circle with a feeling of air in the circle "inflating" the knuckle; this is your "mouth" through which the intervals will speak. The circle never closes enough to touch the A string side of the fingerboard; there is always air in between, when the A overtones are full enough you will be able to see them exciting the open A string. This is even more obvious if you transfer the activity to the C string to play C-D. As the D is a slacker string than the A it will be more easily moved by the first finger D on the C string. In fact both D and A strings should respond to the low first finger D!

If we now look at the intervals making up the C major scale we will see how many notes are rich in overtones. There are indeed overtones in all the notes but because of the nature of the instrument and its dimensions and open strings some notes are richer in overtones than others. C is the fundamental and its octave fourth finger on the G string is easy to check; the upper C should activate the lower open string. D, the next note as we have said will activate the open D. E is not so helpful but can be checked with the open G above (this is a very good argument for learning double-stops at the beginning so we shall come to it as soon as possible). F is again not so easy but it is related to the A. Open G follows and the next note A goes with the open A. B is like E, and goes with the open D, and finally C which we found at the start.

Later on when we are able to play two octaves on the same string it is interesting to discover that we are reasonably at home in the first octave but when we arrive in the higher regions of the second octave we are in unknown territory and not quite sure what is going on. We can get the notes reasonably well because we know the scale pattern, but if we sing the notes to their note names (or sol-fa) we really know what we are doing. How is it possible to search for overtones in these unknown regions if we do not know exactly what note or interval we are playing or searching for? We shall see later how amazing it is to build up overtones on the high notes in the way we have just treated the lower ones, and how gladly the 'cello responds to being treated like this. What seemed to be impossible sounds high on the

C string can soon become an enjoyable experience. This demonstrates in a practical way why it is so important to pulse and sing the note names (or sol-fa) as it is a process of identification.

We now come to a central idea of the "New Approach", that being the fact that it is the articulation of the knuckles of the left hand (the music makers) that controls the automatic swing of the right arm and so the bow. After singing and pulsing the note names of the interval our conscious attention is then directed to the physical manifestation of it in our knuckles on the pulse; the right arm and bow swing in response to this action as an automatic reflex or response. The left hand knuckle, the interval shaper, is the master; the right arm, controlling the bow, is the slave on the pulse.

So returning to our first G-A; A-G interval swing, we see that the swing of the first finger from the knuckle into the A produces an automatic swing into the up bow for the A after the pulse has initiated the first note G on the down bow.

The interesting thing is that when this feeling is fully integrated into the system you will notice that the left hand makes an involuntary movement as though conducting the right arm into the open string. The left hand must lead at all times!

A very important point to notice is that after playing the first ascending interval,. G to A, there is another A to play to start the descending interval, A to G. The danger point is the relationship between the two As. If we take the second A for granted, because it is the note we have just played, it can so easily just be "bowed" and not properly accounted for through the left hand. The first A is produced by the action of the first finger knuckle swinging the finger in from behind. Once the finger is in contact there must be some movement to instigate the second A for the descending interval in the left hand in order to give the right arm its command. The ideal would be to re-articulate the first finger but as this is not possible in legato, the natural thing to do is to put a pulse through the finger in the form of a "give" or "curtsey" by the knuckle. As long as the repeated note receives its command from the left hand the bow will not take on the responsibility and make a bump between the two As.

This leads us to the fact that we cross the strings by way of the left hand and not the bow. It is obvious that the bow does cross the string, as we worked on levels in detail in the last section, but it only works in response to the left hand on the pulse.

After the B to C interval on the G string (third and fourth fingers, see Plate 28) comes the open D. The crossing is initiated by the recoil or springing off by the fourth finger which automatically signals the right arm to swing into the D string level. The fourth finger returns from behind forwards back to the C on the G string signalling the right arm to swing down into the G string level again. The two open repeated Ds are conducted through the left hand above the fingerboard on the pulse.

Always think of the shape the interval makes in the left hand and how it feels to make this shape. We shall discuss the relative interval shapes across the string, and the idea of there being only one large string instead of four separate ones a little later.

When you have experienced the intervals C to D; D to C (fourth finger to open D) and are convinced that it is the left hand that is in control of the operation, we have covered all the basic physical aspects of the "New Approach" as far as the 'cello is concerned. All other facets can be deduced from what we have done so far; shifts, double stops and so on, all refer back to these fundamentals. However, there is a great amount of detailed work to do in reducing all the problems back to the fundamental base and a great deal to think about regarding the mental aspects.

You will notice that in the latter part of the work on the left hand we talked more of the knuckles than of finger tips. This returns to the idea that it is the large parts which control any action. In fact it is the muscles and tendons in the forearm that motivate the knuckles, but as we cannot see these at work too well, it is through the knuckles that the movement is felt, the fingertips are the ends of the action and though the tactile connection with the string is felt there, it is the knuckle that instigates the action.

You will most likely have a strong desire to have a good look at the knuckle action, but the eyes are often responsible for providing misinformation. 'Cellists are not as naturally afflicted in this way as are violinists who have their left hands presented to them right in front of their eyes. Nevertheless 'cellists are liable to get stiff necks craning round to look at the left hand in the lower positions. Fit imaginary blinkers to yourself as the eyes have no function as far as the fingers are concerned.

The eyes tell us that we have a tremendously long fingerboard running down away from us like a motorway. Cut a piece of string to the length of your fingerboard and see how long it is, not more than two feet at the most. It is not possible to make a big shift on such a short length, but even an octave shift can terrify us if we look at the seeming distance downwards. All left hand work is done first by "knowing" the interval inwardly and then working through the tactile sense from the big shoulder joint down the arm, through the knuckle to the finger-tip.

There is one function in which the eyes can play a useful role and that is in the "mime". Before we could talk about miming we first of all had to experience what the left hand knuckles in conjunction with the right arm and bow felt like; it is of no use to try to mime something we have not experienced on the instrument in making the intervals part of you.

Our practice should always consist of five sections in the following order:

1. Pulse (clap) and sing the intervals to the note names.
2. Mime the knuckle movements for the intervals in front of you so that you can see the back of the left hand easily and allow the right arm movements to respond as though you had a bow, and always sing the note names. You will not find it easy at first to achieve the required level of concentration but the mime will eventually enable you to save many hours of wasted practice on the instrument by making the instrument part of you.
3. You can then transfer the mime of the left hand to the 'cello, except having no bow you will make no sound apart form the singing of the intervals. This time you will not need to look at the left hand as the tactile sense has taken over and you will feel the intervals connected to the string.

4. Now, without the left hand, make the appropriate right arm movements on the open strings with the bow to ensure that these movements are organised. At the same time sing the intervals you would have shaped with the left hand. This might be difficult at first for the ear but it will certainly help to strengthen the inner knowledge of the intervals. We will return to this section when the right arm movements become more complex. It should be done at all times, even for the very straightforward right arm movements. Be careful to see that the bow is always working on the string it would have been on when the left hand is in use.

5. Finally, play the intervals on the 'cello, this time only singing inwardly to yourself as it would do no good to compete with yourself vocally. *Your inner voice is now manifest through the 'cello.*

All practice should follow this pattern from these first intervals, through scales and studies, to a concerto. A concerto is only composed of intervals of a scale or arpeggio!

We can probably understand better now what "there is no bow" means, which is an imaginative way of expressing the fact that we are only conscious of a reflex right arm movement in response to the interval-making left hand. If this idea does not do anything for you, think of the bow in the same way you would wear a comfortable favourite garment or pair of shoes. As you wear such things you are never aware of them, but you would soon know if they weren't there. It is the same for the 'cello. There is "no 'cello". If you think about it our listeners never should be aware of a 'cello or bow either. If we say to them in our playing "This bit is difficult" or "This is too fast for me", they will certainly be aware of the 'cello and the bow, plus all your problems. Our problems are of no interest to the listener; their interest lies only in what the music has to say.

To take on the discipline of the five practice sections is, at first, not easy to sustain, but they will eventually help to ensure that "there is no 'cello; there is no bow". Just MUSIC!

Major Disposition

The next step following what we can call the *Basics* (that is, all we have discussed so far) is the two dispositions of the left hand.

In any given lower neck position there are two shapes the left hand can take up. The first one we have already done in the basics, that being the interval of a tone and a half or minor third between first and fourth fingers, which we can call the minor disposition.

The shape which makes an interval of two tones or a major third is often called the Extension. This name itself produces an idea of something *extra* or *stretched*. We hope that we shall be able to experience that this so-called "extension" is just as natural and easy as the minor disposition, so perhaps logically a better name for it would be the "Major Disposition".

We have already experienced the shape of the major disposition in the basics when we discussed the fanning out of the first finger to prepare the note A on the G string (Plate 24). This movement finishes with the hand in the minor disposition, so we must find how to use the fan in the context of the major disposition.

Play G-A-B flat on the G string. Always keep things simple by using separate bows at first going through all the processes, mental and physical, laid down in the basics. If you do this as it should be you will come in from behind to produce the A with the first finger and then even the dramatic semitone to the B flat with the second finger will have a very small "skate" into it from behind and forwards. This is a very subtle small movement but will produce the sadness of the minor form. (Always remember that however small the behind-forward movement is, it is always initiated far back in the shoulder, never locally in finger movement). If in any doubt, play the G-A-B flat mechanically on top of the string without any behind-forward movement to experience the difference in quality. Musically the two ways should be in different worlds.

Now if we continue the behind-forward movement with the second finger to skate it a semitone higher to the B natural, and at the same time allow the first finger to open out, or fan, behind in a single co-ordinated movement, we shall have arrived at the major disposition (see Plate 29).

Example 4

minute slide from behind   larger fan from behind

So the exercise for the major disposition will be G-A (open first), skating into the B flat with the second finger and sliding on a semitone to B natural. Remember the fingers are always rounded into the north-east side of the string, and this goes for the first finger as well, until the moment of release, as the second finger moves from the B flat to the B natural to fan the first finger out.

In effect what we have done is to move the second, third and fourth fingers up a semitone on the fingerboard by opening out the distance between the first and second fingers from a semitone shape to a tone shape. Therefore, physically the second, third and fourth fingers and thumb are in exactly the same relationship to the string, fingerboard and neck as they were in the minor disposition. What is the thumb doing in this operation? It is always rounded in movement with the main part of the hand. In other words as the second finger skates into the B natural the thumb comes with it, or if you prefer it, the thumb motivates it from underneath the neck in a gentle polishing movement. Actually as the first finger fans out there is a very slight forward and inward movement of the whole arm towards the body motivated at the shoulder which is responsible for the fan, and in the process takes the thumb forward and slightly more round underneath the neck towards the C string side. If the thumb remains anchored the upper three fingers certainly will not be in the same relationship to string and fingerboard as they were in the minor disposition. This is an extremely important point and is the main reason why the execution of the major disposition (or extension) often proves a major stumbling block.

What might appear at first to be a slightly different action when using the major disposition is when we play a sequence of intervals on the G string, B flat, C, (second and fourth fingers) to open D finishing on E flat (first finger fanned). The problem here is that the upper fingers (second to fourth) can so easily feel fixed and remain down whilst the open D is played, and finishing on a first finger "poked" out backwards for the E flat. To avoid this static approach play the B flat and C with second and fourth fingers, releasing each as you swing from one to the other, and as we always cross strings at the instigation of the *left* hand knuckles the fourth finger will release to produce the D, but at the same time the hand fans out into the major disposition shape allowing the first finger to curl into the E flat from behind forwards.

Example 5

Later, when this scale sequence of B flat is required at a quicker tempo there will be little time to curl into, and fan out, again on the E flat, so the hand will have to remain in the major disposition catching the E flat on the way through. If we finish on the B flat (a semitone above the open A) then a true feeling of finality would be achieved by rounding into this last note regardless of tempo.

As the first finger is our strongest digit, apart from the thumb, we can ask it to do things that we could not expect the other fingers to do. Already you will know that the fanning of the left hand is achieved by the opening out of the first finger alone, so in this quicker tempo in the major disposition our first finger is somewhat compromised as far as producing overtones curling into the north-east side of the string. However, this ubiquitous first finger is able to discover how to produce the overtones in another way by searching for the overtones on the north-west side of the string (that is the A string side of the D string). In fact the fanned-out first fingertip really falls between the D and the A strings as it nudges the E flat passing from the open D to the F second finger, and on to the fourth finger G through the open A finishing curling into the first finger B flat.

Obviously, there is no difference in the feeling between doing what we just have discussed and the movement in the A major scale between C sharp (fourth finger), open D and E natural (first finger); this being just a semitone higher for the left hand than in the previous B flat sequence. The significant difference is that in the A major sequence the fanning action of the left hand is initiated by the opening of the gap between first and second fingers to achieve the major disposition shape in the true behind forward movement.

Example 6

On the other hand the B flat scale sequence can so easily suggest a "fixed" position feeling at the start as it is not until the E flat is required that the first finger has to fan out to the major disposition shape. The release of the C for the open D and the consequent fanning of the hand for the first finger E flat will ensure that both B flat and A sequences feel exactly the same physically. Always experience the descending sequences after working on the ascending ones to ensure that the fan works naturally in both directions.

The main thing to remember about this sometimes problematical major disposition is that it is not something new to be learned after achieving a natural minor disposition. It is all part of the same process; a natural outcome of the minor disposition. You will soon realise that if you are not blessed with large hands the way to achieve the minor disposition in the first (or half) position naturally is to allow the fan to operate between the first and second finger just a little as required. But the movement from behind forwards will be there to achieve the minor third shape. This will be most noticeable when we come to deal with double-stop thirds. Whether it is a minor or major disposition shape the approach is the same. They are both based on the same principle; the movement from behind forward, the thumb responding underneath and the fanning action giving any distance required without any suggestion of having to stretch.

Chapter 5

Shifts (change of position)

As we are going to talk about various specific positions we had better mention the fact that on the 'cello we are not quite as well organised for naming the positions as are violinists. For instance, is the first finger playing D sharp or E flat on the A string the upper third or lower fourth position? Janos Starker and George Bekefi in their "An Organised Method of String Playing" have categorised positions by semitones which seems to be the most logical way.

Whatever we call each position the important thing is that we know exactly the shape and interval of our move. We must know what our base finger is playing when we arrive; that is, what our first finger (or thumb in the high positions) is playing and how all the other fingers are related, not only on the string we are on, but relatively on all the other strings higher or lower. For instance, if our first finger is playing C on the A string we should know instantly that our fourth finger in the minor third shape will produce F sharp on the C string.

Example 7. Minor Third Shape

All positions, irrespective of what we call them, have relative interval shapes across all four strings and these we must know as well as our own house. This is possible and acceptable in the lower positions, but how many of us can put our hand on our heart and honestly say that when in a high position on the A or D string we know the notes we would produce relatively on the G and C strings? This is a question of learning the intervals and interval shapes and needs discipline.

We now see what the concept of one large string rather than four separate strings means. In other words it is the same experience for the left hand to play C (first finger on the A string) to F sharp (fourth finger on the C string) as it is to play D (first finger on the C string) to F (fourth finger on the C string) because both are minor third shapes. We will feel this even more strongly when we come to double stops.

To move on to the practical physical side of shifts we will find that there is nothing basically new to learn or experience about this subject as we have already experienced the movement from behind forwards with the whole arm from the large shoulder joint when we fanned from the B flat to the B natural in the major disposition exercise. Also we experienced the movement over the whole range of the fingerboard when we were discovering the extended balance earlier. The main difference in practice between the extended balance exercise and actually playing a big shift from the first position to a high position is that the arm will be somewhat lower to start with in the first position. This will mean that the upper bout of the 'cello will have to be negotiated in a way that will not cause the slightest change of attitude in the left hand in whatever position it finds itself. In fact as the arm level is naturally raised as it goes into a higher position, the only change in aspect to the string by the left fingers is that the fingers become *slightly* more rounded into the east side of the string, which is all to the good.

The area around what is usually called the fifth to seventh positions on the 'cello is some sort of "no man's land" and unless we can find a way of preserving a unity of attitude of hand to string all sorts of problems will crop up.

The physical swing that will solve this problem is natural and easy. However, to be able to use this natural movement for our purpose on the 'cello, we have to use two exercises for discovering the thumb position. At first sight this may look like putting the cart before the horse, but without eliminating the physical problem of the large rib of the 'cello, we will be stuck without any way to move freely over the whole range of the fingerboard. So we will have to tackle what is thought to be a more advanced part of 'cello playing in the early stages. In fact the very thought that lower positions are easy and the higher positions difficult creates blockages and problems at the outset. The idea that the lower neck positions are easy is because they are comparatively familiar and conversely that the higher thumb positions are difficult is because they are not so familiar. Surely it is better to tackle this problem earlier than later when attitudes tend to harden into a state which says "thumb positions are impossible". Even when we are convinced by working in the way of the New Approach that the thumb positions are either "easy or impossible" how do we get from the lower neck positions, past the large rib, up to the thumb positions through what we have just described as "no man's land"? The following two exercises are designed to solve this problem.

But before trying them we should think a little about the mental approach to shifts and intervals. As we said earlier, we should convince ourselves that the length of the fingerboard is comparatively small and the biggest shift we could possibly make is not that far, less than two feet! What we must have is the inner knowledge of whatever interval we wish to play. If we haven't, no amount of organisation of the physical aspects will help us. The bigger the interval, the stronger should be our inner perception of the interval and the better will be our physical response.

To reiterate, we should imagine that the fingerboard represents one large string rather than four separate strings. On this we sculpt interval shapes: that is, a minor sixth is a semitone shape from first finger on the lower string to second finger on the higher. A minor third shape will produce a minor third on the same string, or a major third if the fourth finger crosses to the lower string, or a minor seventh if it crosses to the higher string. You will see from this that there are just a few basic shapes, but thinking of the four strings as one, the application of the shapes between fingers in one position to produce musical intervals is legion. Not only should we relate shapes between fingers in one position but relate them to shifts as well. For instance, if we make what is possibly the first shift we learn; D, fourth finger on the A in the first position, to E, first finger in fourth position, would be a perfect fourth shape as far as the distance covered by either the first or fourth fingers were concerned (either B to E or D to G) whereas the actual interval made is just a whole tone. We shall return to this later when we discuss choosing a fingering. From now on always think in *interval shapes*.

Example 8

Whole Tone Shift -
Perfect 4th Shape

Returning to our problem of the shift to the thumb position, we will first have to feel what it is like to be in a thumb position. It is sometimes necessary to use this in the lower neck positions so we can use this fact to learn the first part of the whole movement.

Just as the right arm movements were divided into two halves for the sake of clarity, so here it is better to take each part of the movement separately.

Example 9

Rest and pause for   Rest and pause
lowering arm after repeat   for raising arm

Play the first four notes normally in the fourth position making sure that all the fingers stay in contact with the string for the purpose of this particular exercise, with well-rounded joints and thumb resting in the crook of the neck. Pause after the second B, resting the bow on the string (Plate 30). With the motivation from the left shoulder, slowly raise the whole arm on the balance platform, at the same time allowing the thumb to describe a circular movement, initially backwards, to negotiate the curve of the underside of the neck, then round the edge of the A string side coming from behind forwards on top of the fingerboard until the thumb lies across the notes G and D on the D and A strings (Plate 31). The great danger during this movement is to allow the backward sloping attitude of the fingers and left hand to be pushed forward. This tendency must be resisted at all cost. If the fingers already in contact are undisturbed by the movement, apart from a more sideways contact of the string by the fingertips due to the raised arm rounding the fingers even more, the thumb will automatically sit back on its rear edge.

Now, if you imagine the mid-point of the left forearm as a pivot point for the left hand and elbow, the lightest adjustment from the shoulder joint will enable the thumb to search for the overtones. (This is the balance platform of the forearm operated from the big shoulder muscle by the left shoulder joint). You will notice this later when we discuss double stops because you will be able to adjust the resonance of fifths with this balanced movement. Also you will find that the lower string is actually in contact with the thumbnail but because of the airborne feeling in the whole arm you will be able to resonate the note satisfactorily.

When the feeling of the thumb across the strings feels natural and comfortable, play the D, E, D then again come to rest on the B natural after the repeat. Then go through the whole process in reverse. Motivate the left arm from the shoulder downwards towards your side, at the same time allow the thumb to curl backwards over the edge of the fingerboard in an arc finally coming forward to rest in the crook of the neck once more. This curved stroking action of the thumb is always in contact with the neck and fingerboard which you must try to imagine is made of "satin and silk".

You will also notice how rounded the first finger is when playing the E on the A string and how much on the north-east side of the string is the contact. This is correct and completely in accord with the description of the left hand's high positions on the violin in chapter 4 of *Stage Fright*.

Try the exercise at first without the bow to establish the feelings, being careful to pause and think on the B's in order to prepare the movements correctly.

It must also be mentioned that this thumb position is a semitone shape less than the normal span higher up the fingerboard, a major third shape rather than a perfect fourth, but it does serve the purpose of relating the feelings of the lower neck positions to those of the higher thumb positions.

We will now have to co-ordinate this with the shift in the following exercise;

Example 10

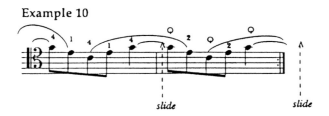

First establish the natural feeling in the fourth position (G, E, C, E, G). Pause and rest on the tied G (Plate 32). The additional movement is now an "opening-out forward" one. The left arm is raised from the shoulder joint and opens out forward with the elbow joint as the thumb, always in contact, is curving from behind the neck in a curve up on top of the fingerboard. This action, though complex to explain, is a natural and co-ordinated one. In fact it is identical to the right arm action except that this one travels forwards slightly more (as in the *swingswang*), in front of you without any sideways component to find the thumb on G and C on the A and D strings (Plate 33). There is even a greater danger here of losing the backward tilt of the thumb and fingers because of the forward movement, but if the exercise is done carefully, at first without the bow, with great attention to this point, you will soon overcome the largest obstacle on the 'cello, namely the large rib which always seemed to block any unbroken progress upwards on the fingerboard.

The descent is obviously in reverse, the arm closing up by the elbow joint, and being lowered by the shoulder joint, the thumb curving backwards and then round to the edge to come forward again into the crook of the neck. You just *fall* back down into the fourth position.

When you are completely at home with these movements you are free to put into practice all the points made in chapter 4 of *Stage Fright* about the high positions. It will be most helpful at this stage to practise bigger shifts of say, octaves, on the same string, either with the same finger or from a lower to a higher finger. This will help to feel the balanced swing of the whole movement. Always remember to keep the thumb flexed and lightly in contact.

You will appreciate how much resonance, and hence natural vibrato, can be gained in the high positions by not pressing down the string on to the fingerboard, but by playing on the inside segment of the string with well-rounded fingers. If contact is made with the string in the plane of vibration it stands to reason that less contact will be required than if contact is made at right angles to the plane of vibration. *Be careful not to overdo this sideways contact so as to pull the string out of line.* Notice the third finger contact is almost the same in the high positions as it is in the lower positions.

Even the thumb, whose contact on the higher string is somewhere just behind the line of the nail bed, and on the lower string is approximately in the middle of the nail, can be adjusted on the balance platform so that the feeling of downward pressure does not exist.

If you have developed a large corn on the side of the thumb with years of downward pressure (and perhaps are secretly proud of it) but would now develop the feeling of weightlessness on the balance platform you would find the hard dead skin would very soon vanish and give way to a much softer area which would enhance the "satin and silk" feeling of string and fingerboard.

In fact the thumb will have to be in contact with the fingerboard, when the fingers are not, because the thumb not being in the plane of vibration requires more contact. This does **not** mean pressure but balanced control from the whole arm, giving the thumb the necessary feeling of movement and air. This is what Kató Havas calls "horizontal energy".

Another particular problem for the 'cellist is the greater distance between the strings. This is especially noticeable when having to play a perfect fifth melodically across the strings. Normally we would play this with a finger flattened across the two strings, but as anyone knows who has experienced this problem, it is almost impossible to achieve a melodic response from a finger locked in this position. You may well ask "what is this to do with shifts?" The answer is that it is possible and desirable to play two melodic notes a perfect fifth apart by moving the relative distance of a semitone shape, using different fingers which can retain the rounded "spongy" feeling.

Take an example; if you wish to play F natural (second finger on the D string) followed by a C on the A string, rather than flatten the second finger across, you can by moving a relative semitone, displace the second finger by sliding into the C from behind with the first finger on the A string.

Example 11

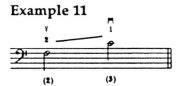

You will feel at once the advantages in the way it is possible to preserve the rounded sponging feeling in the left hand when playing this problem interval. Indeed the very fact of having to perform this small move is a tremendous advantage as it helps to "pulse" the second note more clearly through the left hand. It gives the left hand the movement of command that will co-ordinate the right arm change of bow and string or just send through the pulse more strongly if it occurs in a legato passage under a slur.

A useful preparatory exercise for the "changing fifths" is to play a note (say G on the D string) with the fourth finger, pause, slide into the same note with the third finger, pause, then the second and the first in the same way, and back to the fourth in reverse order. Each note, that is a repeated G, is pulsed with a different finger but the result is identical each time as is the feeling which produces it, is a slide from behind forwards. When this becomes second nature the slide is hardly heard but acts as a connection for a melodic fifth.

As a general rule the more natural way for a "changing fifth" is from a higher finger to a lower finger which produces the behind forward movement required in whichever direction the interval goes, either up or down. It is still possible to go the other way if an ideal solution is not available (see lower fingering in brackets in examples 11 and 12).

Example 12

We will discuss the feeling of crossing the strings with the left hand in greater detail when we come to double stops.

Another possibility for the 'cellist for covering large distances on the fingerboard without formally shifting is the contraction and expansion of the left hand. This is extremely useful for a melodic phrase where a shift may disturb the flow. To give a simple example; suppose you wish to play E, G, F and A flat, starting in the first position on the D string. Normally after the second finger on F you would be faced with a move or extension of some sort, but if after playing E and G (first and fourth fingers) all fingers remained lightly in contact, the first three fingers and thumb close up behind the fourth finger until the first finger senses F in a tone shape. You are now half way to solving the problem, and have the left hand slightly more closed than normal in a whole tone shape and still with the same sponging feeling. Then as you play F with the first finger, the higher three, with the thumb, open out to a normal minor third shape preparing for the fourth to play A flat.

This is a very simple device, particularly if you have already achieved the feeling of the sponge in the palm of the hand, which should never be lost. Also the slight backward tilt must always be maintained to allow the opening out feeling. Of course it is possible to contract to a semitone between first and fourth fingers, lightly pushing the two in between out of the way, and to expand to a major third. The descending passage is the reverse with the upper three fingers closing to the first, then when the fourth is established the lower three and thumb expand again to establish the first.

Example 13

The possibilities of this device are enormous when used wisely, and it is particularly useful in passages containing intervals of consecutive thirds. In quicker passages it is often better to use normal well-chosen shifts but only experience will be a guide as to when to use this device.

Whatever else happens, always make sure that the thumb is flexed and cradles the neck and is always part of the movement whether it is expanding or contracting. It is most important to have established the feeling of a particular note before either contracting or expanding for the next note, otherwise the feeling of security will be lost followed by the consequent anxiety, tension, poor intonation and tone quality.

Example 14. For first finger only on G string

Returning to the lower positions to experience the freedom in shifting, do the exercise which starts from the first finger A on the G string (first finger exercise). First sing and clap the intervals A-B, A-C sharp, A-D, and so on, always remembering that when you come to play it, the note on which you have arrived swings back to the A, so A-B is an interval but so is the B back to the A. A reminder that in this downward interval the first finger, driven on the arm, swings back behind the A each time so that it can come from behind forward into the A. As we come to the A-E the arm senses the large rib and becomes slightly elevated and progressively so to the A-F sharp, A-G sharp, and finally to the A-A. Once again avoid any tendency to allow the hand to tilt over forwards as you go up, always sit on the back edge of a rounded first finger and allow the upper arm to open out progressively as you go higher to avoid any tendency to reach or stretch with the fingers. You will now feel the benefit of the thumb position exercises. Ex. 15 uses the higher part of the previous exercise [ex 14] and is in triple time helping a natural swing.

Example 15: All on C String

There is no rule as to when the thumb comes up completely as this depends upon size of 'cello and player. However, as a guide the arm will be slightly elevated, as we have said, for the E so that the thumb will follow a little way round the crook of the neck on the A string side, and even more for the F sharp. If you find it more comfortable to allow the thumb up for the F sharp, so be it. As always the criterion is physical ease and comfort. As soon as the thumb becomes responsible for distorting the rounded attitude of the fingers in contact with the string, by remaining down in contact with the crook of the neck, it is time for the thumb to come up. This is a feeling you will discover in practice and as a general guide it would be better for the thumb to come up sooner rather than later in order to avoid any feeling of stretch or awkwardness. When we come to the last exercise in this section, the octaves, it is the thumb which helps to drive the whole arm from bottom to top and negotiates the neck with the stroking action as if it were the most natural feeling in the world, "horizontal energy".

The octave exercise [ex 16] is produced by the movement we used to find the extended balance, of which the previous exercises are just the first part without covering the full distance. You will now appreciate the benefit of all we have done in discovering how to shift from the lower to the higher positions by means of the thumb position exercise. The whole left arm swings forward, away and up as in the *swingswang* and back again without the large rib of the 'cello even existing! When such freedom is achieved you will find much joy in discovering the big intervals as the right arm responds to the left in a whole co-ordinated movement.

Example 16: on A String with full bow swings

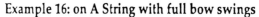

Now that there should be no physical blockage, any interval is possible so long as you are tremendously aware of that interval inwardly. Big interval shifts, small movements in the same position, it is all fundamentally the same, just **know** your fingerboard, and anything is possible!

There are many works available now for the systematic study of positions and relative intervals across the four strings. Whether you use one of these or devise a system of your own it is paramount that you know your fingerboard intimately. If there is a choice between separate or slurred bowing, always choose separate bows at this stage because this will underline the response by the right arm from the left hand articulation. Slurred bowing is treated later in the "Legato" section.

Chapter 6

Vibrato

This subject alone has probably provoked more contention among string players than any other item in the history of string playing. It is perhaps easier to describe what vibrato is **not** than what it is. Once we are aware of vibrato as a separate entity, as something added to the playing process, it is no longer part of the whole and so cannot serve the music.

The main problem, as always, is physical tension. If the sound produced does not satisfy us because of it, we try to enhance the quality by shaking or wobbling the left hand because we see it as the done thing. If the original sound has no life, no amount of shaking will bring it to life!

The clue to the secret of vibrato lies in the production of the original sound and, as in everything else in music, it must be related to the inner pulse. It comes from a movement in which the shoulder, arm, hand and fingers are involved as part of the whole in sponging, softening and rounding the left hand; in fact vibrato cannot be separated from the activity of producing overtones; it is the inner pulse and overtones which control the movement.

If we consciously practise an oscillation which sharpens and flattens the sound whether it be from the whole arm or forearm and wrist, it can only be a matter of luck if it happens to coincide with the sonorities of that sound. Also, of the two, the whole arm has a better chance of control than the forearm and wrist which is at the end of the physical chain and relies entirely on localised muscular control.

When we hear sounds near to the ideal, that is where "there is no 'cello and no bow", it is almost impossible to learn what is happening by what we see. It is rather like watching a magician. The illusion is complete.

With some careful intelligent thought we can discover the vibrato from what we have done so far. There is movement, of course, but there is great danger in being dogmatic in saying such and such happens. The movements are so small and subtle and grow naturally out of the demands of the music, always searching for overtones to produce a shining quality. Whatever the specific movement is, it is certainly generated, like all other movements in the left hand, from the large back muscle through the shoulder, arm and hand to the fingertip contact.

It would be fruitless to say that there is a vibrato for this or that dynamic or this or that composer. There is a quality of sound, which goes to make up a dynamic which in turn suits a particular composer or mood of which vibrato is part.

"There is no vibrato" because it has no life of its own outside the whole sound. It is the result of the combined power of the energised pulse and imagination which shapes our concept of the music. If we have organised the physical aspects in balance well, the vibrato will be there as a focus or prism on which a ray of white light falls and splits it into a beam of colours; overtones!

An exercise which will help to discover the natural vibrato is to play two tied minims in a bar.

Example 17

Play each note with each of the fingers in turn starting with the fourth, that is the fourth finger on one whole down bow and up bow followed by the third and so on to the first.

On the first two pulses on the down bow set up all the balances normally making sure the left arm and hand is still, with no movement whatsoever. In other words in an ideal state of balance with no energy being sent through - **passive**. On the last two pulses as the right arm swings out to the point send the energy through. This will set into motion the search for the overtones by the left hand, that is the sponging, rounding and softening of which vibrato is part - **active**. If any noticeable effort creeps in causing tension, stop, and as always let the arm hang by your side to allow the tension to run out of the fingertips.

Notice that in this exercise the passive part is on the shorter part of the right arm movement, i.e. heel to middle by balance, and the same on the up bow, point to mirror middle by balance. The active part is done when the right arm is opening out and accelerating towards the end of its swing. This is the ideal response to the active or alive left hand as the energy is sent through. Remember as the movement in the left hand is small, the difference between the active or alive part of the action and the passive or restful part of the exercise is not very great. Also the alternation between the two ensures that it is difficult for tension to build up as the passive part is like a soft cushion on which to rest between the energy-charged sections.

Only do this exercise in very short sessions with a great deal of concentration and awareness as vibrato has to grow naturally, and always constantly nurtured.

Chapter 7 : (part 1)

Double Stops

The word "stop" is unfortunate as we do not want to stop anything. We hope that what we want is to start overtones vibrating. However, as "double stop" is in common usage we had better stay with it. Double resonance might have been better.

There is a thin line between pleasure and pain which is so often drawn through the execution of double stops on a stringed instrument. Nothing gives more satisfaction and pleasure than a satisfactory double stop passage, and how much enjoyment you can get by playing a duet by yourself. We need not dwell on what happens on the other side of the line when tensions build up and music dies on the battlefield of frustration.

Maybe it would not be so foolish in an ideal situation to start beginners with double stops, rather than single notes making intervals, because they would feel the interval shapes in the left hand immediately. To be at all successful the left hand would have to take up the attitudes we have already discussed in single note intervals.

Many factors are responsible for happy double-stop playing and the primary one must be to achieve a sonority on both notes which blend with one another so that each note helps the other to produce more overtones. Imagine what tension does! Exactly the opposite and battle commences!

Perhaps it is relevant here to digress for a moment to think about how a good chamber ensemble, or any group of string players including orchestras, can achieve a satisfactory balance and ideal sonority.

Take an octave or unison passage, if all players played their individual part at the same strength and sonority as everyone else the chance of building overtones would be slim, but if, say, the first violin decided that he would "sit" more lightly on the resonance made by the second violin both would be aware of the overtones each were producing. Similarly for the viola and 'cello; the viola would rest on the 'cello resonance and the result would be two pairs of two players being aware of one another's resonance. When this happens the outcome is quite something. To produce real magic all the players concerned would have to have a capacity and understanding to put into practise all that we have been discussing and searching for so far.

This is what we must look for when we play two notes together on our own instrument. It all comes back again to what goes on in the mind; a strong knowledge of the two notes inwardly and the interval shape they make in the hand.

The work on double stops is simple and specific. They fall into two main categories, one is the sixth and the other is the third.

All other double stops fall into one or the other category, as will be explained.

Let us start with the more straightforward one first, the sixth. On the 'cello we normally start in C so we will take the first interval of the scale in sixths, E and C. First sing and clap the interval E to C and then discover E on the C string by playing the interval C (open string) to first finger E and back again to C. Play the first finger E with a swinging up bow and with a very strong articulation from the second finger base joint bring in the upper C on the G string with the down bow sounding them both together. Make sure the strong second finger articulation does not induce a forced accent or a harsh quality, which is often the case when playing double stops for the first time. Round and soften and, at first, only look for a soft "piano" silky sound. The right arm will sense the combined level of C and G strings on the down bow so as to produce a balanced sonority as it feels the lower C string level first, and then swing towards the G string level in response to the second finger articulation of the upper C.

Example 18

That the feeling of the double stop interval shape is based on the lower finger is fundamental to successful double stopping. It is better that the bow brings in the upper note on the down bow as this is a part of the natural swing; if in doubt try it the other way round! Also playing on two strings at the same time would seem to produce a flat plane thus tending to flatten out the curve of the bow stroke. This need not be as there is enough flexibility in the two strings to respond to the curve of the right arm swing.

To summarise: if the lower finger (in this case the first) is on the lower string (C) the upper note is brought in to be played together with the lower note on the down bow. Everything is based on the lower note in the sixth interval, both arms sensing the E on the C string, and then the upper C is tuned in by the second finger coming in from behind forwards as the right arm responds. You should now begin to feel the idea of one large string rather than four separate ones. When you are happy with the double stop E C it would do no harm to release the first finger on the E to check the second finger C's resonance with the open C. This interval E-C makes a semitone shape.

The next interval, F-D, second finger on the C to fourth finger on the G, is done in exactly the same way. Notice how much fan is needed as you round into these notes. The first finger will be way back and the thumb well underneath the neck. All that we have said about producing overtones on single notes will have to be done many times amplified in double stops. As we said, always start with a soft "piano" approach; the forte will come later by sending more energy through and spread chords can be broken down into double stops before attacking them head on. We will deal with chords later in this section.

We must not forget that when we play two double stops one after the other that there is a connection between the two. In the case we have just looked at the "glue" between the two is the second finger which swings down a fifth from the C to the F to become the new base finger for the F-D. It is always more difficult to achieve a legato join in a case when the same finger has to jump a fifth in the same position across the strings. This calls for that much more of a swing to get a legato than would just single notes and if we were dealing with single notes we could resort to a "changing fifth" which we discussed earlier. The upper part of this double stop pair is no problem as the fourth finger comes from behind for the D as the second finger swings over for the F. Mentally it is this move to the F with the second finger which is in sharp focus, otherwise there is no base for the fourth finger to come from behind into the D (see Ex.18). This interval makes a whole tone shape.

The next interval is more straightforward as the second finger F swings from behind into the first finger G on the C string; the upper notes are fourth finger D to third finger E on the G string. So from the double stop F-D (tone shape) to the double stop G-E (tone shape) we have a tone shift between them. It is essential to have a clear mental picture of all the shapes and moves between them. What is true in a more straightforward single melodic line is even more so in a more complicated passage.

A good idea for helping the awareness of the connection of double stops is actually to sound the lower finger, whether it be on the lower or upper string, just "fingering" the higher finger without sounding it. The bow would be on the lower finger level all the time. This will focus attention on the vital function of the lower finger on which a double stop passage is based. It does not follow that the lower finger is always playing the more important note harmonically or melodically, but physically it is all-important.

Always remember that very often a series of double stops *are* two melodic lines, or at least one melodic line with an accompaniment.

If we are not aware of this we can so easily play a series of double stops as though they are rows of separate boxes on a shelf. Mentally we tend to isolate each double stop because we see it like that on the music, the left hand responds accordingly and the right arm responds to the left hand with heavy pulled accents and battle commences once more!

If we change key to C minor the first degree would be E flat to C making a tone shape between first and second fingers (major disposition).

Returning to the major form we have already experienced E-C (semitone shape) F-D (tone shape) and G-E (tone shape). After this comes A-F third finger on the C string and fourth finger on the G string (semitone shape). Then the next one is B-G (semitone shape) just a fifth above the first (E-C) double stop, this, like the lower one, is back to first and second fingers on the G and D strings. Next comes C-A (tone shape) second and fourth fingers. D-B which follows uses the first open string in the sequence, open D to first finger on the A. Had you remained on the G and D strings for this one, which might not be a bad idea if just doing one octave, you would find it was a tone shape. Finally E-C (semitone shape) done with the first and second fingers on the D and A strings (see Ex. 18)

If we list the shapes of the degrees of the major scale in sixths we get:- semitone, tone, tone, semitone, semitone, tone, tone, semitone. You will notice that Degrees I, IV and V are semitone shapes. So the degrees on which the primary triads are built are semitone shapes and all the others, minor and diminished, are tone shapes; so a strong harmonic feeling helps to define interval shapes in the left hand.

Moving on to the other main category, thirds, we will find this pattern is the same except that the left hand shapes are now major or minor thirds. It is interesting to note that all the actual major intervals on I, IV and V are produced with minor third shapes, and all the minor third intervals are produced by major third shapes. The simple fact is that if we play a minor third interval on the same string it is produced with a minor third shape, but if we play the same minor third interval in another position across the two strings it will be produced with a major third shape, and vice versa for the major third interval.

Why is it necessary to make two categories of double stops? Once we begin to put thirds into practise the reason will be clear.

As always sing and clap the intervals. This time in the third interval C-E, the E is the higher note and as in the sixth E-C the E is played with the first finger. So again it is not the tonic note C which the left hand senses as the important note for it to function from strength; but it does mean that this strong powerhouse from behind allows the other fingers, including the fourth, to function without tension. Should we function from the fourth finger first there might be a tendency to tense, and as nearly all thirds in lower positions are played with the first and fourth finger, it behoves us to nurture our fourth fingers! If ever we need a left hand free of tension it is when we play thirds.

Which of us can put our hand on our heart and honestly swear that we have not felt any tension whatsoever across the back of the hand and knuckles when playing an extended passage in thirds? How can we overcome this problem?

For reasons just explained sing and clap the third interval C-E from the upper note first, E to C and then from C to E. Discover the E, first finger on the D string by tuning it in to the resonance of the open G. No doubt you will be surprised how sharp this E can be; it is a disease of the first finger to be sharp in the first position! We will return to this point later in this section.

Now with a full slurred up bow play E in the first half, and with a strong articulation from the knuckles allow the second, third and fourth fingers in a co-ordinated unit to come from behind forward into the C on the G string in the second half of the bow.

Example 19

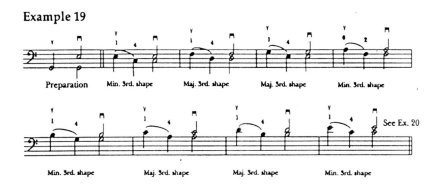

Preparation   Min. 3rd. shape   Maj. 3rd. shape   Maj. 3rd. shape   Min. 3rd. shape

See Ex. 20

Min. 3rd. shape   Maj. 3rd. shape   Maj. 3rd. shape   Min. 3rd. shape

Example 20

Min. 3rd. shape   Maj. 3rd. shape   Maj. 3rd. shape

Although it is the fourth finger which actually plays the C the involvement of the two middle fingers is vital. If they are not part of the whole movement they can so easily stick out horizontally or remain raised above the string, and when this happens just look how the skin over the top of the knuckles is stretched and white; visible tension! So all you have to do is to release the tension in these two knuckles and allow them to help the fourth finger to do what it has to do. We have done all this before when we were discovering the interval shapes at the start of the section on the left hand. In this case the minor third shape is over to a lower string rather than on the same string but if we are thinking of one large string a minor third shape is a minor third shape!

Another point about the feeling of unity in the left hand is that if these two middle fingers are not involved in the third shape, whether major or minor, we are left with a first and fourth finger, like a pair of dividers stuck on a map, but with no feeling of the distance (shape) in between. These middle fingers are vital in feeling the shape of a third - the whole hand involvement. Although this first interval is a minor third shape you may find that you will have to allow the gap between the first and second fingers to fan a little, as you do when going to the major disposition, in order not to stretch or strain. This is true, of course, when playing a minor third interval on the same string.

The feeling as you play the E-C in the slurred up bow is that the right arm responds to the upper part of the left hand (second, third and fourth fingers) coming into the G string like a soft lump of butter or lard landing "splat" into the note C. If ever you need the soft and silky feeling you need it now; *get rid of the bones in the left hand!*

Now the bow has arrived on the lower string you can play the C-E as a double stop in exactly the same way that you played the sixth on the down bow.

You can now see why we have to divide double stops into two categories. In the first case, sixths, the lower finger and right arm level are both on the lower note. In the second case, thirds, the lower finger is on the higher note so we have to play the two notes separately to allow the right arm to reach the lower level before joining the two in a double stop. Seemingly a small point, but very important in order to achieve balance, thus making it possible to be free of tension. We can find the feeling of the next interval in the third scale, D-F (or F-D as we shall use it), in exactly the same way as the first, except that this minor third interval will be a major third shape. Anyone who has had a problem with the major disposition will have to come to terms with it now as a scale in thirds is totally composed of changes between the minor and major disposition. In a way the shifts or "glue" between each double stop third are perhaps a little less of a problem than in the sixths because, apart from an odd open string, the upper notes are all first finger shifts and the lower ones fourth fingers. In the higher positions the pattern is between thumb and second finger, and first and third fingers alternately (see Ex. 20).

It is the opening and closing of the fan between first and second fingers which controls the major and minor shapes of the thirds. As in all double stops, but particularly in thirds you must know the shape of each individual third and its relation to the next one. You will realise the validity of this when you come to learn the melodic minor form!

If the double stop interval is unsatisfactory, tension will follow automatically so rest immediately. So often when attempting to play two notes together we struggle on manfully trying to put it right, but it only gets worse, the reason being that we have lost our point of reference physically and aurally. Stop, break off! Allow your arm to rest at your side and allow the tensions to run out of your fingertips on to the floor. When you are sure they are gone, and only then, start again basing the left hand on the lower finger and finding the right arm balance on the lower string before bringing the two notes together again. This simple action demands no small amount of discipline as the natural feeling is one of anxiety to conquer the problem. Always remember to produce double stops softly at first so that you can search for the overtones clearly.

All double stop intervals fall into one or the other category. Fifths can be taken like sixths although as these have to be played by the same finger or thumb they will have to fall into the gaps between the strings, that is catching the lower note on the north-west side and the upper on the north-east side. Higher up the instrument the finger may have to be flatter or more horizontal to cope with a slightly wider gap between the strings, although the thumb can be used on occasions for a fifth in the higher regions. It is all a question of adjustment and balance. See the remarks in the section on the thumb position about changing fifths.

Perfect intervals do have to be perfect, fourths, fifths and octaves all have to resonate with the optimum of overtones, whereas the imperfect intervals, sixths and thirds, have a small amount of leeway depending upon their musical function and can be coloured accordingly. Discords, seconds and sevenths, etc., need even more attention than concords. The overtones need discovering in both notes and then coaxing into working together to herald their resolution.

As an example resonate the E, first finger on the D, with the open G string (up bow), and on the down bow bring in the D, fourth finger on the A. This is a minor third shape playing an interval of a minor seventh. For a moment release the first finger E to resonate the upper D with the open D below. When you are happy with the resonance of each note, develop the spongy rounded feeling in the left hand to make the two notes of the discord work together instead of pulling harshly against one another. As you do this, imagine what the resolution is going to sound like, the D falling to C (second finger on the A) while the E remains. A little work on these lines, with a soft quality, will show you that a discord need not be harsh aurally or physically.

The fifths, played higher up with the thumb, across two strings have been touched on in the previous chapter in the thumb position section. As we said this is done by using the whole arm in balance so that the hand and elbow balance one another from the mid-point of the forearm all suspended from the large back muscle and shoulder joint. If splitting up the fifth by playing the lower note first, as in the sixths, does not produce a perfect interval, adjust by allowing more balanced weight on to one or the other of the notes until the interval is indeed perfect. This is a more successful solution to the problem than twisting the thumb around to find the fifth.

Octaves are often looked on with apprehension, but if we do what we have done in the previous double stops they will begin to respond very happily. Normally any extended octave passage will be played by the thumb on the lower note and the upper with the third finger. Like the feeling of the interval of a third the intermediate fingers help to release any tension by resting behind the third finger to give the feeling of a whole unit, which also helps to get away from any isolated thumb and isolated third finger stuck on the strings. Trying to play octaves like this is next to impossible as there is no point of reference and it degenerates into two notes, which are virtually the same, chasing one another like a dog chasing its own tail. It would be advisable to start octave practice in a high position so that physically the interval shape in the left hand would be compact with the thumb across the D and A strings on the half harmonic node. As this double stop is in the sixth category, play the low D with the thumb on the up bow and bring in the upper D on the A string with the third finger (helped by the first and second in a rounded whole) on the down bow played together. It is more important with octaves, than perhaps any other interval, to realise that the powerhouse, which comes from way back in the shoulder, transmits its power to the lower finger; in this case the thumb, whilst the upper note, the third finger sits *lightly* above. When this is really organised it is as though only one note is being played rather than two. Be careful not to apply on-top pressure to the thumb, but allow the arm's balanced weight to produce the D and let the higher fingers trace the octave shape above. (see Chapter 8 : Artificial Harmonics, examples 22a and 22b).

When you come to put the octaves together in a continuous passage, just play the lower note with the thumb, the bow only on the lower string, but at the same time trace the pattern with the upper finger silently. This is essential for all double stop practise of all categories and interval shapes as it makes sure that the power source is being driven through the lower digit from behind forwards.

A danger in doing the above exercises is that, after playing the separate preparatory notes, there is a tendency to "pull" with the bow as the two notes are brought together as a double stop. This is brought about by a quite natural feeling of wanting to help make a point that these are in fact two notes together; anxiety again! Also if we are not too keen on the result we get when the two notes come together, the bow accelerates to get over the problem quickly and get on to the next. The solution is to remember the right arm swing response and to aim for a quiet, soft feeling in both the left hand and right arm to search for the overtones.

Spread three and four part chords are approached in exactly the same way as double stops, as each chord can be split into either of the two categories. As an example we can take the four part C major chord; open C and G, E (first finger on the D) and C (second finger on the A).

The right arm senses the level of the two lower open strings.

Next take the open G on the up bow bringing in the E, first finger on the D string in the down bow to check the G-E. Finally do the same for the E-C semitone shape double stop on the D and A strings played with first and second fingers. After establishing a good relationship with the G and E you are left with the overall shape in the left hand of a semitone E-C. Before putting the whole chord together we should experience the movement in the right arm. Sometimes it happens that the spread across four strings can induce a feeling of wanting to wrap the bow hair round the strings in the same direction as the curve of the bridge, which produces a dull, heavy, staccato bark. In fact the movement is still in a curve opposite to the curve of the bridge just as if playing on a single string. Now if you imagine the one large string instead of four separate ones you will be able to adjust the curve accordingly. Try this first on all the open strings to get the resonances flying upwards out of the 'cello. The outside of the upper arm senses the levels of the C and G, the G and D and the D and A in one co-ordinated curve.

Now introduce the control on the pulse with the left hand semitone shape E-C. It is modern convention to play the lower two notes as an appoggiatura before the first pulse and bring in the two higher notes on the first pulse, so in this case the first and second fingers conduct the chord and the right arm responds. The feeling is that the semitone shape E-C catches the pulse on the D and A strings. Incidentally, notice how far back the first finger has to lie and what a big semitone shape it feels. Sometimes on a large instrument it may be necessary to open out the gap between first and second fingers a little to find the natural resonance, just like starting a move towards a major disposition. It would be a good idea to adopt a quaver pulse for a chord of a minim value as this gives plenty of time for the final two notes to resonate.

It is important in chord playing that two notes at least are always resonating together (unless otherwise indicated). Because of the curve of the bridge it is not possible to have more than two notes sounding together but there are subtle differences which can be introduced to chord playing. For instance if we play the open C and G and immediately steepen the curve to go straight into the upper notes E and C, the chord would have a feeling of finality. On the other hand, if we were to flatten the curve in the right arm a little and dwell on the G-E in the middle of the chord for a fraction, it would produce a chord more suitable for starting a piece. In fact the Sarabande of the Bach C major Suite has exactly this same chord, one to start and one to finish.

Another aspect of chord playing is the release when all of the left hand is involved. In the case of say the D major chord played with the first finger taking the low fifth D and A on the C and G strings, and the third and fourth fingers taking the F sharp and D on the D and A strings, we shall see how it works.

The problem is that we often want to hang on to the low fifth when we go over to the F sharp-D, thus clamping the whole hand down in a block.

To be successful we shall have to release the first finger from the D-A fifth as we catch the F sharp-D underneath the neck. The first finger is fanned out to help the natural spread of the semitone shape F sharp-D in one co-ordinated movement. Chords do look like blocks visually so this movement is vital in chords to bring them to life musically. A very good example is at the start of the second section of the Sarabande in the Bach G major Suite. The first three-part chord D- A-F sharp is a preparation for the next one which is the same with the C added. The first fifth, as we have found, is done with the first finger between the strings and comes over towards the G string side to give more A as the F sharp comes in. Before trying to play the four-part chord work on the top two notes C to F sharp semitone shape. Notice that this comes into the "third" category. Lower finger (second) is C, to higher finger (third) is F sharp. When you know the feeling you are aiming for at the top of the chord you will be free to release the low fifth. Do not forget this upper pair is based on the second finger C which is the higher note. Only experience of feeling this will give you absolute confidence with such chords.

To recapitulate the ground rules of double stop practise:

1. When the lower finger is on the lower string play it with the up bow separately then bring in the upper note to play it together with the lower one on the down bow (see Ex..18).

2. When the lower finger is on the higher note, play the lower finger to the higher finger in a slurred up bow as separate notes, and bring them together as a double stop on the down bow (see Ex 19).

Chapter 7 : (part 2)

Arpeggios and Scales

It would be a good idea to look at the problem of the Arpeggio in this section. What does an arpeggio have to do with double stops and what is the problem? The problem is that arpeggio intonation can be notoriously approximate and the solution could lie in the use of double stops to help.

The reason why arpeggio intonation is likely to cause problems in the early stages is that they are made up of larger intervals than scales, initially demanding more of us both aurally and physically. This causes us to be either tentative or anxious or both. To overcome this we must sing and clap the intervals as always, but amplified. The greater the interval the greater the *inner pulse song*.

Example 21: arpeggio study

Example 21 demonstrates how the interval shapes mould the left hand through the use of double stops. The sixth interval E-C gives the left hand a positive semitone shape in each octave preceded by the shift C-E to establish it. The problem interval is the perfect fourth G-C, C-G. Most of us would get quite a surprise if we were to check this interval on a regular basis when playing arpeggios normally!

By finding the perfect fourth tone shape in this way (it is the "third" category) you will feel the nature of the interval, and notice how much fan it requires. The tendency is so often to stretch, particularly when the G is played by the third finger in the two higher octaves. A well executed fan will allow the third finger to round into the G and notice how much the second finger playing the higher C has to be rounded to allow this to happen. This exercise can be extended to include the seventh of the chord (in this case B flat) turning it into a dominant seventh chord of F. So now all the major and minor arpeggios and dominant seventh arpeggios are at our disposal!

The diminished arpeggio needs a slightly different approach, although the *inner pulse song* needs super-amplification both for this and for chromatic scales. The diminished chord is a series of minor thirds, beloved of composers for changing key. In the lower part of the arpeggio you will notice that the left hand is making major third shapes to cross the strings, but then contracts to a minor third shape when on the same string, so a series of alternating major and minor third shapes are made "backing" across the strings until you come to an open string or can go no further. The relative distance covered between these openings and closings is of course a semitone and are all done between fourth and first fingers. The action is rather like the ripple of a many-legged insect, a centipede, as it traverses the ground. The secret is not to release the fourth finger until the first finger has fanned out to curl into the higher note. As this happens the fourth is released and as the first curls into a minor third shape the fourth is ready to articulate the minor third on the same string. The process is repeated until the A string is reached. The opposite is true of the descent. The first finger fans out to allow the fourth finger to make a major third shape on the lower string; as this happens the first finger curls in from behind to make a minor third shape on the same string and so on to the end.

The upper octaves are usually played by a sequence of first and third fingers up and down the A string. An intelligent organisation of the first octave, i.e. whether to start with a major shape across the strings or a minor shape on the same string, will ensure the right grouping of the high octaves. If the start is not right you will finish on a third finger on the penultimate note which either means another unnecessary shift or an awkward extension using the fourth finger in a high position.

The only section of the scale gamut we have not touched on is the Chromatic. This is not really anything to do with double stops, apart from checking with an open string whenever possible, but for the sake of completeness we can deal with it here.

The accepted way of producing the semitone intervals is by just using the first, second and third fingers with one move on each string between the two groups, the fourth being reserved for finishing a sequence if appropriate. Anyone coming to a chromatic scale for the first time will know how easy it is to get lost in this uniformity; for some reason when the open string arrives it refuses to fit the chromatic pattern!

The solution to the problem is, as always, the inner pulse song. The two main groupings of the chromatic scale are either four groups of three or three groups of four. If we use the latter first you will be amazed how some singing and clapping in semitones Pa, Pa, Pa, Pa - Pa, Pa, Pa, Pa - Pa, Pa, Pa, Pa - Pah (octave) will ensure that any open strings are well integrated into the chromatic pattern and the final Pah will be an octave above the first note.

The only department we have not considered in detail is the straightforward diatonic scale, although we did this when we were learning the first intervals at the start of the left hand. Nothing could be better for practise at a slow tempo than taking out each ascending step, repeating the upper note to descend again on every interval G -A, A-G. We will deal again with the grouping and the faster tempo of scales when we deal specifically with "fast" playing in a later chapter.

Before leaving the subject of playing two notes together we should touch on the subject of tuning. Tuning in the wider sense is such a vast subject that we can only touch on it as it applied to a stringed instrument.

There are many varied ideas about how to tune a 'cello, but if we rely on the feelings we have discovered so far we have already solved most of the problem. In searching for the C major chord we have found the balance on the two lower strings which can be transferred to the other two pairs of strings. As the natural movement in music is from behind forward, that is from lower to higher, it is better to arrive at a perfect fifth by lowering whichever string you are tuning and bring it up until it resonates with the string you are tuning to. Usually it is the A which is the point of reference. So you would bring up the D to match the A, the G to the D and the C to the G. As what you have done at the bottom will slightly affect the tuning of the upper strings it is usually necessary to do a second fine tuning before all the fifths will be satisfactory.

Tension will make tuning difficult. It is the *fly* part of the preparation for the bow stroke that will give you the lightness and balance which is so necessary for producing the clarity of the perfect fifth and it is the "after ring" when the right arm curves off the string which gives you the clearest aural vision of the fifth. There must be a clear light balance between the two notes, both being equal in strength and much better to have a "piano" quality.

If we are happy with the tuning of our instrument and all pairs of strings are resonating in perfect fifths there is an interesting feature to consider which can be demonstrated in the following way. Play the open G string with an up bow and with the first finger coming in from behind to play the E on the D string and bring both notes together on the down bow to play the sixth G-E with a satisfactory resonance. Without moving the first finger play the E on the D string by itself on the up bow and bring in the open A above to form a perfect fourth interval E-A as a double stop. You will realise immediately that this interval is far from perfect, in fact it will need raising a detectable amount before it will resonate with the open A as a perfect fourth. So the fact is that the E with the G is not the same note as the E with the A.

This demonstrates what is often termed the "comma" in the octave and why it is necessary to "temper" the tuning on a fixed instrument like the piano. We are free on a stringed instrument to enjoy what is called "just" intonation. This does not mean a free-for-all; far from it. But on the other hand it would not serve the purpose of a musical performance if such discrepancies were worked out in the minutest detail-a sort of "tempered" performance on a stringed instrument. There is a school of thought which suggests rather than tuning our A to the piano A we should tune our G to the piano G at the same pitch. This would tend to bring our middle range more in line with the "tempered" piano.

The problem is there, but it is better to rely on one's innate tonality to colour the imperfect concords, sixths and thirds, appropriately in whichever key you may be. As far as resonances are concerned on a stringed instrument we have to be guided by the resonance of open strings because they are always there resonating to a greater or lesser degree, perfect intervals are just that-Perfect! A strong harmonic feeling is essential if we are to solve intonation problems met in playing chamber music. In each key through which the music passes, the Tonic, Sub-Dominant and Dominant (I, IV, V) are "static". All others are adjustable. If we try to raise or lower anything arbitrarily, to try to make a "fit", we create insoluble problems for ourselves. When in doubt in extreme keys, flat keys are slightly higher, and sharp keys are slightly lower than might be expected. Within this structure is the ever-moving kaleidoscopic interval shapes which make music. The history of the problems of tuning is a long and interesting one and anyone who has the interest to follow it up will benefit in understanding.

Chapter 8

Harmonics

As the subject of harmonics is central to the understanding of how sound is produced and how a string vibrates, it would be of great benefit to be familiar with, first of all how they work, and secondly how they can serve the music.

The following is offered as a simple guide as to how we can discover the usable harmonics available.

The A string is used as the example to be split up into its harmonics, but naturally each of the other three strings can be treated in the same way.

There are two main types of harmonics, natural and artificial, so we will start with the natural harmonics.

A natural harmonic is obtained by touching the string at the required position, called "node", very lightly with the finger; but we will discuss the practical details later; first the facts.

If we divide the string into two equal parts we get this picture:

Ex (A): half (1/2) harmonic

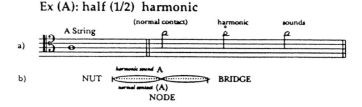

(The normal contact note is always bracketed, and the node numbers are counted starting from the nut end upwards to the bridge)

If we make a normal contact at this node we get the note A, an octave above the open A and only the part of the string between the finger and bridge is fully vibrating, but of course if it is being "sponged" and "softened" in the way it should be, the sonority will be vibrating many other parts of the instrument also.

However, if the contact at the node is of the lightest, it will produce a true harmonic; in this case the half (½) harmonic which provides the same pitch as the normal contact (see Ex. A). This allows the other half of the string between the finger and the nut to vibrate freely also.

Obviously the next step is to divide the string into three parts to produce the third (1/3) harmonic : -

Example (B): third (1/3) harmonic

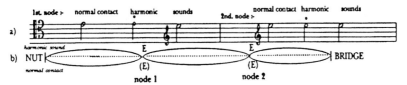

The first node produces the E harmonic, an octave above the normal contact. The second node gives the same pitch both as a harmonic and a normal contact (see Ex. B).

The fourth (1/4) harmonic is : -

Example (C): fourth (1/4) harmonic

In this case the second of the three nodes is the half (½) harmonic again, so the pitch A the other two nodes produce is an octace above the half harmonic in which these higher notes are included but concealed (see Ex C).

At first sight it may be puzzling as to why the last node (number 3) is not producing D on the normal note like it does on the first node. If you think about it the normal note on the third node is vibrating a quarter of the string between the finger and bridge which gives A, also the harmonic is producing that same quarter, which is also exciting the other three quarters between finger and nut, all producing A. However, when the normal contact note is played on the first node the first quarter is no longer part of the vibration, so there is no longer an equal division of the quarters remaining to vibrate; in this case three, which produces D. This principle will be seen to operate again in the following examples.

The fifth (1/5) harmonic is: -
Example (D): fifth (1/5) harmonic

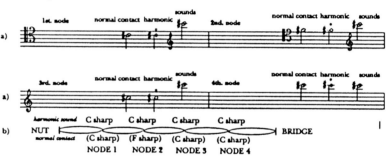

The harmonic on the first node is two octaves above the normal note. On the second node the normal note is F sharp and the C sharp harmonic is a fifth plus an octave above it. The third node has the normal note on the C sharp with the harmonic an octave above it. The fourth node is C sharp both on the normal note and the harmonic at the same pitch (see Ex.D).

The last really usable harmonic is the sixth (1/6).

Example (E): sixth (1/6) harmonic

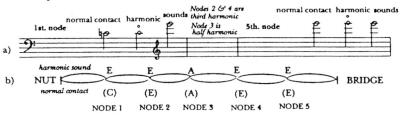

The first node does not respond so easily at first to its harmonic, a major third plus two octaves above, sounding E. The way to help it is to find the last node (number 5), which produces the same pitch on the harmonic as the normal note E.

When you have produced the sound required and assimilated it, go back to the first node on C natural and you should find something interesting; it still will not produce the required E until you move higher, just a whisker. Try this a few times until you are happy going from the highest to the lowest node, coaxing it to speak clearly.

There are two factors at work here. One is that because you have a clear idea for what you are searching in your inner ear by finding the E in the last node (no. 5) near the bridge, you can find the E in the first node (C natural) with much greater certainty.

The other is that because that string has been divided into six parts from the top node, it appears to respond more readily if you go immediately to the lowest node. It is as though the string has "learned" how to divide into six parts.

Remember to go on the high side of C natural!

The second and fourth nodes are of course the third (1/3) harmonic in which the sixth harmonic is included but concealed, and the third node is the half harmonic again in which are included and concealed the fourth (1/4), the sixth (1/6), and the eighth (1/8) harmonics. (see Ex. F)

With all this encapsulated in the half harmonic, it is now possible to see what an important part the harmonics (overtones) play in producing a vibrant, living sound!

The eighth (1/8) harmonic of course divides the fourth (1/4) harmonic into two, but some of the divisions, such as the first node around B (first finger in the first position) do not readily produce the required A, consequently it is better to find this high A in the highest node near the bridge.

The following harmonic series (see Example F) is based on A, two octaves below the 'cello's open A, and shows from where these particular harmonics are derived.

Example (F): harmonic series of A

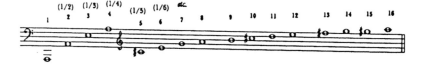

These are the usable natural harmonics but we also have artificial harmonics available., artificial, because they no longer rely on the natural division of the string to produce the harmonics.

If we make a perfect fourth shape on any string in any place, making the lower digit contact the string normally but the upper one as lightly as in a natural harmonic, it gives us a sound two octaves above the note the lower digit is contacting. If you look at the fourth (1/4) harmonic (Ex. C), the nut to the (fourth finger) D at the first node is a perfect fourth interval and shape which produces two octaves above the nut (open A), when played as a natural harmonic.

From this you can see why the perfect fourth shape will always produce the double octave above the lower digit.

Normally it is better to obtain the perfect fourth shape between thumb and third finger, which is also the octave shape across two strings. The playing of artificial harmonics has exactly the same problems as octaves (see Ex. 22b) and should be studied in conjunction with them.

The main difference is that the third finger really does have to trip the light fantastic in the way it makes a ghostly trace of the lower pattern that the thumb is shaping. If it is an extended pattern of artificial harmonics the only way is with thumb and third finger, but for a few notes it may be possible to play them with a fanned first and fourth finger, the first finger having the normal contact and the fourth the lighter contact.

Unlike natural harmonics, whose nodes are always to be found between equally divided sections of the string, artificial harmonics by their nature demand that the perfect fourth shape becomes smaller, relatively, as they travel higher on the string just as with octaves. Obviously this is because the string is only vibrating effectively in front of the thumb and as it goes higher the string becomes shorter. (see Ex. 22b). This type of harmonic responds more readily on the longer length of string. The shorter it gets the less likely it is to speak.

Example 22a produces the high E which is the same as the natural sixth harmonic (see also study 59, *Etudes du Jeune Violoncelliste* - Feuillard)

Example 22a: artificial harmonic

Example 22b

In all harmonic playing the right arm has a very important function to play. As the left hand is in charge and has to learn the tactile lightness of contact, this feeling has to be transmitted to the right arm so that it can respond to this light movement. If the "whole" is not working, however well the left hand may be coping, the harmonics will not ring clearly.

How do harmonics fit into a musical context?

Like open strings, harmonics are often thought of as an embarrassment because they are not "warm and living" like a "stopped note".

The unfortunate term "stopped" is with us again and is partly the cause of this particular misunderstanding.

If we are indeed "stopping" notes and using a heavy wide vibrato, and suddenly out comes a clear harmonic or open string, then they will stick out like sore thumbs. However, if the general sound is vibrant and rich in overtones, open strings and harmonics will fall in place quite naturally given that they always serve the music in a particular context. The best place to hide a pebble is on a beach! (Listen to any recording of Emanuel Feuermann).

At one time there was a fashion to edit out open strings and harmonics from Bach's string music by using the higher positions. As we have just commented, the shorter string will not resonate as readily as the longer string and Bach, of all composers, was fully aware of the resonant possibilities of the instrument he was writing for, so why not enjoy the resonances of the open strings and overtones he provided?

In some of the lighter salon pieces, such as the famous
Boccherini Minuet, the use of the half harmonic is inevitable, in fact
the whole of the first section rings with the half and third harmonic
(see Ex.23). However, this must be done with extreme lightness and
good taste. The analogy of the skater is really appropriate here; the
light movement of the whole arm skating from behind forward
taking the third finger to make the lightest contact with the node of
the half harmonic is like a bird alighting for a moment and taking
off again to land on the fourth finger, F sharp, to continue the
passage (bars 4, 5 and 6).

Example 23

A useful characteristic of the natural harmonics is that they will
ring on for a time after the finger contact is released, which is just
what is required in this case as it gives the arm plenty of time to swing
back to come in from behind for the F sharp, E, D sharp sequence
while the harmonic A seems to be suspended in mid-air.

This is a very well-worn trick of the trade and if overdone, or
done in the wrong place can be flippant and tiresome; but done in
the right way in the right place is a delight.

A composer who understood how to use harmonics to good
effect in all departments of music was Ravel, and most of his string
writing contains well-written passages in harmonics, as for example
in his Sonata for Violin and Violoncello.

Chapter 9

Trills and Ornaments

Musical ornamentation always tends to look less significant when written down than the main notes it is embellishing.

In practice exactly the opposite is true, the small notes, whether they be trills, appoggiaturas, accacciaturas, mordents, or turns are all of the greatest significance. Their exact interpretation is up to each player to discover for themselves. Musicologists are far from agreeing on this subject, but if we take into consideration the history of a particular composition, the era in which it was composed and the nature of the music the grace notes are enhancing, we should be able to come to a conclusion which fits the music naturally on our instrument. Many ornaments are vigorous, disturbing accents. In slow movements, care is needed not to be athletic.. As in all that has gone before, ornaments must be part of the whole musical flow on the pulse. Whatever the ornament or grace note, we must inwardly understand its function and relationship to the main notes in the phrase, and to the pulse.

First attempts at trilling can be one of the best ways of inducing tension in the left hand and because of this sudden intense activity the pulse goes out of the window too!

If we do what we did when discovering the first intervals we have the answer to the problem. The articulation of the base joints from behind forward and the softening and sponging of the left hand is providing the movement for the trill but at a greater frequency. Because of the greater frequency the movements are that much more economical, i.e. much nearer to the string. Basically though, the movements are identical to those of the first interval shapes, the coil and recoil. (see Study no.1 in the Appendix).

Example 24

The spring and recoil action from the knuckles.   Always feel at rest on the longer note.

The exercise (Ex. 24) will help to develop this feeling as a preparation for the trill. Now use the vibrato exercise (Ex. 17) to trill on the second of the two tied minims after remaining passive on the first. Use an inner pulse of quavers so that you are trilling on the last four pulses in the bar and make the last quaver pulse stop the trill so that you will have a fraction of clear note on which the right arm swings into the up bow to the next passive note to prepare again for the trill on the last four pulses of the up bow. The process at the point is repeated at the heel. Start at first with semitone trills above the first and second fingers. Notice how the intermediate fingers work to help in the tone trills (see section on double stop thirds). The stopping of the trill on the eighth quaver pulse by the left hand in the exercise is important particularly when we come to trills on dotted notes. If the trill gets out of control of the pulse and hangs on too long it will cloud the clarity of the dotted rhythms. We will go into dotted rhythms in greater detail in the next section.

The trill, normally being an embellishment which happily generates energy, is full of light and air which is the feeling we use to produce it.

In the lower positions the feeling is very much underneath the neck with the thumb, as though you were catching something soft in the palm, so that the fingers being articulated through the knuckles can coil and recoil sending the trill upwards out of the instrument like sparks off an anvil. Never consciously try to trill quickly as this will immediately seize up the left hand; just allow the fingers to coil and recoil through the knuckles on the pulses, always remembering that the lower finger on the main note is soft and spongy just as though it were playing without the trilling finger above. There is a great tendency to hang on with this finger because of the trill activity, thus causing tension.

The inner pulse will dictate the speed of trill, like flutter or ripple from underneath. You will be able to transfer this feeling easily to the high positions.

As we have said, the grace notes look so small written down but the articulation to produce an appoggiatura or accacciatura is tremendous. In quicker tempi, these notes along with the mordent are incipient trills and an accacciatura often starts when the upper note is required first. The appoggiatura is often half of the full value of the main note and is often an accented passing discord, so the articulation of this is of great interest and importance in its relationship to its main note. In general first discover the bare bones of the musical structure on the pulse and then integrate the ornaments as part of that structure.

As with everything else in musical performance, the concept of the music and especially the grace notes, trills and turns must be strongly conceived inwardly before attempting to play anything. Always go through the five preparatory exercises (in Chapter 4).

Chapter 10

Pizzicato

Specific guidance on this subject is so often wanting that individuals looking for help are left to improvise their own solutions.

If all the foregoing has been well understood and absorbed, common sense will lead us to a true understanding of how pizzicato can be executed.

As always, the left hand is in control (on the pulse) as the interval maker, the right arm responding accordingly, but this time as there is no bow, it is the fingers of the right hand which resonate the string.

Take up a balanced posture with the 'cello and swing the right arm into the normal balanced attitude (see Plates 7b and 7c), with the index finger rounded into the north-west side of the G string, and allow the arm to open toward the extended balance attitude, say to a point about two-thirds the length of the string to the bridge. The point of contact made by the finger will be varied of course, depending on the nature of the timbre required by the music in the same way as the bow approaches the bridge or the fingerboard as required.

Allow the thumb to contact the C string edge of the fingerboard; let us see what happens if we just pluck the G string, making sure that the thumb has just the lightest of contact with the edge of the fingerboard. Each joint of the index finger will flex as it curls into the north-west side of the G string. The initial finger contact on the string is by the fleshy pad below the fingertip and, apart from special effect pizzicato, is of a soft velvety feel; the object being, as always, to produce the greatest amplitude of overtones (see comment in chapter 2) with the minimum of physical effort - a clear bell-like sound.

The actual finger movement is locally initiated by the knuckle joint. However, if this is done as a whole musical movement you will notice that it is the large shoulder joint again that really instigates the movement, just as in the small swinging "nudges" to play the quavers (PA -PA's) with the bow. So there is nothing new or different in the fundamental movements. Normally the swing, as with the bow, is in the side-to-side plane of vibration on a shallow curve which vibrates the string from side to side. Occasionally a composer asks for a special effect in pulling the string upwards away from the fingerboard and allowing it to snap down on it with a harsh crack.

Decide on a moderately slow pulse and pluck the G string twice and notice how the thumb with the whole arm swings away after the first pulse to return on a swing back for the second pulse, and so on; if the tempo is quicker there will be less time to swing away but the feeling of swing is there, even though the thumb remains in contact.

There is, of course, the same level control in the outer edge of the upper arm when changing to other strings just as if the bow were being used.

It is when the pizzicato is in use that the work of producing true resonance with the left hand is most appreciated, otherwise the effect can be so dull and dead. As pizzicato is such a short transient musical experience compared to the legato, the left hand has such a comparatively short time to produce the resonance required, so consequently it must "sponge", "round" and nurture the notes immediately on the pulse so as to give the pizzicato its alive, bell-like quality. Also, because of its transient nature, pizzicato can so easily degenerate into the playing of separate notes rather than musical intervals. It is always a good idea to check through a pizzicato passage with the bow just to feel the sonority and interval shapes.

Occasionally the second finger is preferred to the index finger to pluck the string, but this changes nothing fundamentally. There are certain pieces of Spanish or Latin-American origin which ask the player to imitate the guitar either in chords or single notes.

Sometimes the single notes are large quick-moving intervals of, for example, tenths. In such a case the thumb swings in on the arm catching the lower notes on the north-east side of the lower string, to swing back allowing the index finger to round into the north-west side of the higher string and so on to the thumb again. This action is, as always, motivated by the shoulder joint with the whole arm in balance and can be likened to the escapement action of a clock.

The same action is used for chords and normally it is the thumb that swings into the lower note and curves upwards through the higher notes from lower to higher in a connected arpeggio. Again the overall movement, as with the bow, is in a curve opposite to that of the bridge. Sometimes it is possible and necessary to produce a chord in the opposite direction, with the index finger coming into the higher note first, and finishing on the lowest, but this is an instant swing with the minimum of perceived speed. This is often done with chords alternately to achieve a guitar effect. The movement is identical to that described above for single notes with the index finger, but obviously a much greater movement on a fuller swing.

A problem in pizzicato is that there is often no time to put down or pick up the bow, in which case it must be retained in the hand in some way. If the full connection is maintained, the index finger can be opened out from the connection to the bow a little and used to pluck the string, but there is no thumb contact with the edge of the fingerboard with the right thumb, so extended passages may cause problems done this way. The alternative is to cradle the frog of the bow with the second, third and fourth fingers in the palm, which leaves the thumb and index finger free to operate more or less normally, but it does need a little time to get the bow re-connected again for a following legato passage. The musical content will be the guide as to which approach to adopt.

It is possible for pizzicato to be the cause of tension to build in the right arm when the same passage played with the bow would not be a problem. It is only by understanding the nature of the balances and how to use them in pizzicato and "knowing" the intervals through the left hand that tension can be banished.

Chapter 11

Legato - Staccato - Dotted Rhythms
Legato

"Smoothly joined together" and "to be connected" are defini-
tions of legato with slightly different shades of meaning. To be
connected both mentally and physically has been our aim and work
from the start.

In practical terms we have already covered legato playing when
we first connected intervals in the section on the left hand. But
learning to produce isolated intervals is just the first step, putting
them together in a whole musical phrase or movement is another
matter.

In all art contrast is the device which creates interest and holds
our attention. Total uniformity will usually send us to sleep.

So the term legato is not exactly what it seems on the surface.
In a legato phrase everything is not connected to everything else in
an even uniformity. If we take a simple eight-bar phrase we come
to the end at the cadence before going on to start the next phrase,
and there is usually a breathing space after the fourth bar, these being
the natural punctuation marks of music.

Music is on a constant flow from somewhere to somewhere else,
so in a legato phrase it is for us to discover the natural punctuation
marks and connect the "bits" accordingly. To connect everything
together smoothly in a uniform way would destroy the sense and
shape of the music. We will touch on this again later in the last
section.

For the present all we need to do to produce legato is to reiterate
the fact that the left hand is in charge on the pulse and the right arm
swing responds to it.

When notes are slurred together we have to decide how many

it is musically feasible to cope with in one bow swing at a particular tempo without being inhibited in any way. It is interesting to note that when the bow swing is used naturally, that is being aware of the middle by balance as the true half way, many more notes can be slurred together than if a "flat" bow were used with the measured middle as a reference.

You will notice that the second half of the true swing from the middle by balance to the point can almost feel endless and can more or less cope with any number of slurred notes you wish for, within reason.

Sometimes it serves the legato nature of two notes to change bow instead of slurring them together, as the strong articulation from the left hand should get a big swing response from the right arm tending to connect them more strongly than if they had been slurred. This is particularly true in the case of a string crossing between two notes.

Apropos of this we should perhaps mention a subject we touched on earlier, that of the changing fifth. Rather than squash a straight finger across two strings to play a legato interval of a perfect fifth, come in from behind to play the second note of the fifth with a lower rounded finger making a semitone shift. For example you could play the fifth G to D with the G, fourth finger on the D string; to the D third finger on the A string (see examples 11 and 12).

The feeling is that the rounded third finger comes from behind\ the fourth finger to slide into the D on the A string as a semitone shift. How much better is the legato preserved by this device rather than the straight finger which is not able to produce the overtones in any degree. Another advantage of the changing fifth move is that the articulation of the shift gives a positive direction to the right arm swing.

If the strings on your instrument are near enough together in the lower neck positions it is possible to negotiate the fifth with the same rounded finger by catching the lower string on the north-west side and the higher on the north-east side with the finger pad between the two. In the higher thumb positions this will not always be possible so the changing fifth will have to be used but there are certain passages when a straight finger across the strings is the only solution, for example, the double-stop passage in the first movement of the Saint-Saens A minor concerto.

We have dwelt on the fifth interval because it is the interval which breaks up a legato passage more than any other interval. This is particularly so on the 'cello having the greater distance between the strings than in its smaller relatives, the viola and violin. The "EE-AWE" or "donkey bray" sound of a fifth across the strings is characteristic of the straight finger, particularly if the bow has a say as well, so it is well worthwhile considering the possibilities of how to get round this ever-present problem.

Successful legato playing is simply to reproduce a smooth melodic line without disturbing the shape of the phrase; discovering the "glue" between the notes and their relationship to one another; no 'cello, no bow!

Staccato - Detached Notes

Just as the magician produces illusions, we have to produce the illusion of the short notes which we call staccato of which there are many forms, to create varied musical impressions.

Why illusion? If we think about it a staccato sound is just a legato sound lasting a very short time, followed by silence, but having all the quality expected of a longer-lasting sound. In fact it needs even more quality to make an impression because of its brief life. It needs to speak instantly being full of the life-giving overtones to produce clarity. How is this done? Again we have already done the parts, they just need bringing together.

Probably the most useful type of detached short strokes for the 'cello is the repeated quavers (or semiquavers, depending on tempo) which generally accompany melodic lines, PA-PA-PA-PA, etc., called thrown spiccato for quavers and sautillé or saltato for semi-quavers. (See Study no. 8 in the Appendix).

You will remember looking back to the section on the right arm that this was the first movement we discovered for the right arm in balance as the bow rested on the point of balance, PA-PA, remembering that this is still legato. All we have to do now is to put the left hand in charge on the pulse.

We can use the first octave of G major starting on the open string. Having a strong inner quaver pulse play G-G rest, allowing the bow to rest on the string as this is still a legato exercise.

Then play A-A driving the right arm nudge through the left hand's first finger knuckle. Continue in the same way up to the G, fourth finger on the D string resting between each PA-PA. If you have the feeling of this working well notice what happens as you play the open string; the left hand not being ostensibly actively involved will automatically make a small "conducting" movement to assert its authority over the right arm, so the left hand is still in charge through the pulse even on the open strings!

Now to the staccato. Do this exercise again but this time winch up the height of the right arm a fraction by using the large counterweight in the shoulder blade so that the PA-PA arcs just connect with the string at the lowest part of their curve. As we did previously, make sure the left hand is still conducting the operation on the pulse. But this time, during the rests, allow the bow to swing up to the near vertical position each time saying a strong "AND" on the two quaver rests, as this will prevent us from "hovering"; that is holding the bow horizontally above the string which will cripple the little finger. When you are happy with the two grouped PA-PA's try four with the rests between and finally the fours without the rests. At this stage it would also be a good idea to do the three groups PA-PA-PA-and, PA-PA-PA ,etc.. Notice how the right arm response is now down and up alternately on the first of each group.

It is interesting to notice how you finish these exercises, if you just finish with four G's, musically you are left up in the air as normally four staccato quavers finish on a longer note following. They need a long G to finish in the following bar. If you have really felt the left hand controlling the operation you will have no difficulty in going straight from the staccato quavers to the last long G because, as we have said, there is no fundamental difference between staccato and legato, one being a shorter version of the other. However, if you have for one second tried to bounce the bow consciously and allowed it to take over control, you will have an impossible task going from one to the other. Similarly if you were to vary the pulse a little whilst doing the four groups there should be no difficulty as long as the left hand is in charge; quickening gradually and slowing down gradually.

There comes a speed which is too quick to allow the bow to leave the string on its tiny arc. We have reached the quick semiquaver pattern which, if executed by a living left hand, will give the illusion of staccato sparks off an anvil.. Always remember in this type of spiccato (sautillé) *that all right arm movement is generated in the large back muscle and manifested by the shoulder joint, all other movements there may be, such as in the wrist, are very small cushioning reactions to the whole movement;* remember the quicker the pulse the smaller the right arm movement, which is economical but extremely significant and effective.

The next type of short note we should look at is the martelé. Looking back to the right arm section you will remember that we started this subject with the legato form, the détaché. The right arm movements are for the upper part of the bow to the point, where the arm opens out from the elbow as far as it needs to swing the bow to the point and then folds behind to initiate its return on the up bow; the *swingswang* of the upper part of the bow and, as always, is controlled through the left hand articulation.

Using the G major scale again, play the détaché stroke at about crotchet equals 60 with a full crotchet on each degree. When you are happy that the left hand is in control, try the scale again playing each degree as a quaver followed by a quaver rest, and as in the exercise in the chapter on the right arm, pulse in quavers which will be quaver equals 120. Play on the odd pulses and rest on the even ones. Finally, to achieve the true martelé reduce the played note to a semiquaver followed by the required rests. The right arm movement will be that much more economical than when doing quavers, but still use the area that goes right out to the point. If you ever needed the left hand to control an operation you need it now!

It is so easy to allow the bow to take over in the martelé. When this happens we get what has been described as a "skidding bump". The only solution is to ensure that the left hand produces a semiquaver alive with overtones which produce a bell-like "ping" as the right arm swings out in response. There is a simple study suggested in the Appendix (Study no. 2) suitable for détaché and martelé.

The flying spiccato is more often to be found in the realms of the virtuoso literature for the instrument, and one could be forgiven for thinking it should be left to the exceptionally gifted who do such things as easily as they breathe. Therein lies the solution to the problem, unless it is easy it will not happen. There is no way you can make it work. You can either ride a bicycle or else you fall off.

How then is it possible to learn this trick which seems to belong only to a chosen few? We can find the answer in what we have done so far. First of all the left hand, through the knuckles, must be in charge totally and as always we must have the series of notes, which make up the intervals, very strongly inside us so that we can direct the knuckles in flying spiccato. A series of notes is played in one direction of the bow and written in either up or down bow. The problem is how to control the natural springiness of the bow through the right arm. What usually happens is that we are so mesmerised by this right arm action that we leave the left hand to look after itself and take its chance, but of course the opposite should be true.

Probably the most well-known piece for the 'cello to use flying spiccato is the Boccherini Rondo (Ex 25).

Example 25

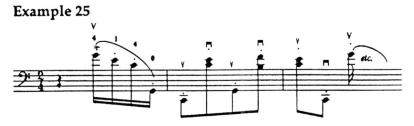

If we go through all the preparatory exercise, singing, miming and playing the relevant open strings at a fairly gentle pace, we should have a very strong idea of what the G-E-C-G-C feels like. In the right arm section of the preparatory exercise on the open strings notice that there are two impulses on the A and one on each of the other three strings. At the slowish tempo you will be starting this exercise there will be no feeling of the bow leaving the string. Start well beyond the middle by balance (towards the point) with the direction being in the up bow. Use the upper arm area in the back edge of the upper arm to find the A string level, allowing the right arm motivated from the shoulder and in balance to describe two tiny arcs with a rest between them; A rest A rest. This is entirely legato and at no time does the bow leave the string.

Now allow the outside of the upper arm to find the D string level, the G string and finally the C in the same small arcs. Do this again in one co-ordinated movement at a slightly quicker tempo and then you will be able to feel the whole right arm movement adjusting to the varying levels automatically. Depending on tempo, the movement in the right arm will start higher or lower on the bow. At first you will need plenty of space being in a slow tempo. You may need to use two thirds or three quarters of the whole bow length. As the tempo is increased so the movement is condensed as you go through the point of balance on the last C.

If we take Example 26 on the open D or A string we gauge the distance towards the point of balance on which we can easily control the last legato note on the down bow. We initiate the inward movement (up bow) with the arm level fractionally above the string to catch the first semiquaver on the bottom of its arc, and like the flat stone which we can skim across the still water, the other three semiquavers follow automatically. Notice that at the end of the first full crotchet, down bow, the arm swings through and the bow leaves the string a fraction in order to swing back to allow the left hand (or pulse if it is an open string) to energise the first of the four semi-quavers. The whole arm feels the strong legato swing in the opposite direction (down bow). The danger of course with "throwing" the bow is that if it becomes a vertical throw the bow bounces out of control and relationship to the pulse is lost. The feeling is of a totally horizontal movement and the spring in the bow "skims" the last four semiquavers without having to do anything except to close the arm in a natural up bow. This has no chance of happening unless the PAH-PA, PA, PA, PA, PAH on the pulse is very strongly inside you (Ex. 26).

Example 26

Continue this exercise using each left hand finger in turn to feel the pulse controlling the knuckle, i.e. E, EEEE-E and F, FFFF-F and so on.

To return to the Boccherini Rondo and take over the pulse in the left hand we would find that if we try to throw the first G we would be in trouble. In this case it would be advisable to establish poise and balance with the right arm connected to the string through the bow to initiate the movement in response to the demand in the fourth knuckle of the left hand. After that the bow springs off to come into the left hand's first knuckle, demanding E and then the outside of the right upper arm says D in response to the fourth knuckle playing C on the D string. Finally the levels in the upper right arm swing into the open G and C.

This is one co-ordinated movement and is more complex of course than the exercise on one note on one level. It depends on the context whether the first note is thrown or not. As soon as you try to put the phrases of the Boccherini Rondo together you will appreciate the necessity of having the control and poise of that first G on the A string.

The next time it comes after the opening is after the open C, so the fourth finger needs all the controlled response it can muster at that moment. To ensure that this works, go through the exercise we did on the open strings but now the control through the left hand G-E-C-G-C is enormous as this springboard will ensure that the non left-handed notes, open G and C, carry on as strongly on the pulse.

It is the *fly* part of the right arm with the left hand in charge, and the overall feeling of lightness and air that will bring success. It is a dance!

Dotted Rhythms

Was it not Wagner who said "Look after the short notes and the long ones will look after themselves"? Why is it necessary to single out dotted rhythms for special attention? Because it is one of the aspects of music, particularly in string playing, which so often lacks clarity.

There are a number of reasons for this. Very often we are not aware of the inner pulse strongly enough. For instance, in the rhythm in Example 27 we are happy to pulse quavers and even crotchets. If we pulse quavers we have more chance of relating the short semiquaver to the next dotted quaver correctly as it comes between the second and third pulses ("and"), but if we choose a crotchet pulse the gap between the pulses is so great anything could happen to the relative values; we could even degenerate into a triplet rhythm. The only sure way is to go for the inner pulse; semiquavers:-

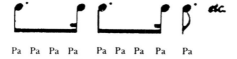

Pa Pa Pa Pa   Pa Pa Pa Pa   Pa

then you will **know** the value of the semiquaver. Of course there are stylistic variations of the dotted rhythms but first we should know the rules before we are free to break them.

Another reason is that our eyes see a series of long notes followed by shorter notes which sends all sorts of erroneous messages to the right arm. The tendency is to make the short note staccato with a short "hump" from the bow and the longer note a "skidding bump" as the bow pulls. This is a picture of the worst case, but however well organised we are there is still a tendency to allow the bow to do "uncontrolled" things with dotted rhythms.

Again the solution is simple as it has its roots in what we have already done many times before. The left hand is in charge on the pulse!

As an example look at Example 27.

Example 27

Generate a pulse in semiquavers at about semiquaver equals 120. Sing and clap the example and go through the whole process as usual to mime etc.. To enhance clarity make the dot in our example a rest. At first sight the rest may look longer than it is, but if we realise that the sound after the second pulse carries on until the fall of the third pulse (the rest) there is just a little daylight between this and the fall of the fourth pulse. The first finger pulses the first three semiquavers on A and commands the right arm to finish its swing on the third pulse to rest in balance until the inception of the fourth pulse for the semiquaver A, and then on for the same for the B with the third finger. This brings about the strong connection between two notes, the final fourth pulse semiquaver A and the first of the next three pulses into B. It is this connection that is the "motif" of the dotted rhythm, so that is the interval with the strong "glue" holding it together; the *short* note followed by the *longer* one. As we said, the eye sees a long note followed by a short one which is the convention of written music.

If we control the right arm by the left hand so as to give us the little bit of daylight between the third and fourth semiquaver pulses, we help the process of making the glue between the short and long notes, thus obtaining tremendous clarity for the dotted rhythms.

If we look at "Studies of the Young 'Cellist" by Feuillard, study no. 10 shows this clearly (see Appendix). The note values are double that of our example but the process is identical. Musical shorthand often uses dots to mean things that can be easily misinterpreted. The dot over the short note in this study indicates a tremendous clarity and not a staccato. The interpretation is clearly stated in Feuillard's explanatory note "Execution". The dot lengthening the first crotchet becomes a rest and the dot over the quaver is cancelled. The dots cancel out one another.

This little B minor study (no. 10) is ideal for our initial introduction to dotted rhythms. So that nothing has to be disturbed it would be better to start up bow so that we would finish down at the end. Like the notation the eye sees the bowing written "up-up", "down-down" etc.. But musically it is "up-down"—"down-up", etc., over the bar line, which is exactly what the left hand should be demanding. The "up-down" has the "glue" of the short note followed by the long one, between it, as does the next "down-up". This type of bowing for dotted rhythms is probably the most common, but there are many other types of bowing possible and, of course, many other types of dotted rhythms. Study no.11 in the Feuillard book is a Siciliano rhythm which is more complicated than the simple time of no. 10.

We have not discussed the nature of a musical motif yet, which for our purposes merely means the smallest number of notes which when grouped together make musical sense; the building bricks of music. In the case of a siciliano rhythm the motif would be

However the eye sees

etc., but it is the second, third and fourth quaver pulses we hear making up the motif. This is a large subject which we will come to again at a later chapter. It is the nature of the motif which tells us which bowing and fingering to choose. The answer is always to be found in the music (see Appendix). Another type of dotted rhythm in compound time is :-

[last movt. Death and the Maiden].

At the request of the left hand, the right arm performs what we discussed in the section on martelé. These movements are small and economical, opening out the elbow slightly, and inwards and behind on the up bow swing; miniature *swingswangs* at the point. When this is working naturally in balance, through the left hand, you will find the crotchet is slightly shortened so there will be just a little daylight between the long note and the next short one, heightening the clarity. The above rhythm can be done at the point of the bow when the tempo is quick. Alternatively it can be done with great clarity and control as :-

at the point of balance whilst a violinist might choose to do it at the point, as in the last movement of Schubert's "Death and the Maiden" quartet. Always remember that when we talk about bowing and its direction either up or down, we mean an *arm swing initiated at the shoulder and controlled on the pulse through the left hand.*

Chapter 12

Interpretation

Apart from the theatre, music is the only art which consists of the trinity of composer, player and listener which, by its very nature, makes a very subjective combination. The dictionary definition of interpretation is " The performance of a piece of music, or the like, according to one's conception of it".

"According to one's conception of it" seems to give us *carte blanche* to do as we think fit, as the whim takes us.

Unfortunately this is what so often happens, particularly in an age when self-indulgent "free expression" is seen as a desirable facet. Do we hear the ego raising its ugly head again?

As we said in an earlier chapter, it is not your feelings and emotions that are of interest, it is the feelings and emotions of the composer that our listeners have the right to experience.

For the executive musician the ever-present problem is how to allow our listeners to experience the composer's music without getting in the way.

The solution is specific and simple. We have said that music is a powerful force to which a composer becomes connected so that when we, the performers, also become connected to the flow our listeners automatically become connected as well. There is nothing esoteric or mystical about this, it is a fact which every musician or music lover has experienced at some time in their lives. When we pulse, singing and clapping the intervals, we have taken the first and major step. After that follows a never-ending development in a musical treasure hunt. One never arrives at a "definitive interpretation", it is always a search for what serves the music.

The greatest and most obvious clue to interpretation stares us in the face. It is often the case that we do not "see the wood for the trees" and in this case it is the nature of the pulse and interval of which we may be aware but do not often realise its significance.

We are exhorted to conjure up imaginative mental pictures regarding certain pieces of music to stimulate our own (and so our listeners') imagination. This may work initially but it is likely to wear rather thin with overuse!

What should really fire our imagination is the nature of the relationship between pulse and interval. Mozart has his own way of relating them, Beethoven another and Bartók yet another. If, in the process, imaginative mental pictures are conjured up all well and good; this is the better way round!

Even the same composer hardly ever produces the same pulse-interval flavour. Take Mozart's overtures to *The Marriage of Figaro* and *The Magic Flute*. Both allegros have quick-moving quavers. In *Figaro* the quavers bustle in a close small interval movement which ooze busyness and intrigue. In *The Magic Flute*, after the introduction, the quavers start hammering away, without interval on the same note, jump into a little semiquaver turn sending the quavers off again into an excursion of arpeggiated intervals. It just bubbles with expectation, like children waiting for the pantomime to start.

Two very different and subtle moods have been evoked entirely by the nature of the pulse-interval relationship. All worthwhile music has its own built-in clues as to how it is supposed to go!

One's instrument itself can bar the way to progress. If the instrument becomes one's obsession then the music takes a back seat. The 'cello, because of its wonderful sonority, is particularly prone to the danger of the seduction of its players and listeners by its own character, often to the detriment of the music. It has not been unknown for tenors with wonderful voices to suffer from the same disease!

If you have a tremendous love and enthusiasm for music you will be avidly interested in everything the music is doing and saying; this should be evenly balanced with the love of your chosen instrument. Allow this balance to be upset in favour of the instrument and the music will most likely suffer.

Mozart's musical message, most readily perceived in his operas, and to be found in all of his music, is as valid today as the day he realised it. The basic and fundamental human emotions, the whole range encapsulated in this music, love, hatred, happiness, despair, jealousy and so on, have not changed over the years but have adapted to surroundings and circumstances.

So to suppose that the works of the great masters are part of an archaic past and are part of a dead language is to miss the point completely.

Like the fairytale prince in the Sleeping Beauty it is our responsibility to re-awaken these works in our day with the understanding of the composer's emotions in his.

It is therefore important to nurture a wide interest in music and the musical scene generally. It means finding a composer's background, the age in which he lived, or lives, and acquiring the idiom and "flavour" of his composition. When we have gained some experience in tasting the flavours of various composers' works, naturally those we are attracted to, our musical intuition will be fed on this. It is not really possible to understand Mozart's quartets unless you are familiar with his operas!

However, our musical intuition can be severely coloured by outside influences and we need to look carefully at how we can use the fundamentals of music to help us avoid the pitfalls.

Before we do that we should look for more clues which will guide us to a true interpretation in a wider field before we come to the details of the structure of music.

What are these clues? First of all there is a tradition which can come directly from the composer in various forms, but we have to be cautious with tradition as we must be sure that it is authentic. Like the "whispering party game", the fun of which is having the distortion of the first whispered message compared with its final form as it reaches the other side of the room (the famous army message "send reinforcements, we're going to advance" becoming "send three and fourpence, we're going to a dance"), tradition can similarly distort the composer's intentions.

A classic case is perhaps the best-known solo ever written for the 'cello, Saint-Saen's "Swan" from the "Carnival of the Animals". Ever since Pavlova used this piece to accompany the dance which she

116

called "The Dying Swan", it has been published and played as Adagio and has been dying ever since. The plus side of this is that Pavlova brought this gem to the notice of more people because of her dance than would have been the case if it had only been heard in context. However, if we look at Saint-Saen's original score, the Swan is marked *Andantino grazioso*. If we believe that the composer's intentions are of paramount importance we will have to treat tradition with suspicion unless we are certain of the facts, and only a "hot line" to the composer could assure this.

So what is the difference between *Adagio* and *Andantino grazioso*? The conventional Italian terms used universally by composers, apart from the occasional nationalistic rebellion, are important guides as to the tempo, style and general flavour of the piece, but in no way can indicate a specific tempo or style, so *Adagio* or *Andantino grazioso* could be less far apart than first impressions might imply. Experience will tell us what *Adagio* is and what *Andantino grazioso* is in a specific case; they have their own very characteristic flavours, the difference of which is not entirely due to tempo.

It is only when we start digging a little deeper into the structure of the music that we can come to any valid conclusions. Looking at the piano part it does not need too much imagination to realise that it represents the water on which the swan glides. The harmonies are not rapidly changing and the time signature is 6/4, implying an overall two pulse with an "inner" pulse of crotchets or even quavers. All this suggests a particular kind of musical movement.

The natural movement of the solo line is not quite as it looks written down. We see the first group as G, F sharp, B and the second as E, D, G then the long A in the second bar. In fact the first G belongs to the water flow in the opening bars of the pianos which creates a flow over the bar line. Then the F sharp, B, E is the next cell or motif with B flowing into the big fourth interval E. Then D, G-A again flows over the next bar line into the long A and on to the quaver B to the final C of the first phrase. The bowing does not have to follow this motivic pattern, in fact if the bowing follows its normal shape of three crotchets to each bow in the first bar the change of bow on the swing between the B and the E will highlight the shape of the perfect fourth, given that the left hand is leading as it should, and the same for the tone shape G to A over the next bar line (Ex.28).

Example 28

Notice the practical use of the changing fifth between the D and the G (second to first finger).

Apart from choosing a fingering to suit the musical flow, we have covered most aspects of the interpretation of the first few bars of the *Swan*. It is desirable to specify a tempo for this particular *Andantino grazioso* so we can usefully call on the much maligned metronome for help. As we have now acquired a "taste" for the Swan we can try an area on the metronome we think would fit, perhaps somewhere in the region of crotchet equals 88 would have enough movement. We will be covering the structural aspect of a musical phrase in more detail later on.

But for now what have we found out about Saint-Saen's *Swan*? By sensible detective work, that it must have flowing movement, and the composer overtly indicates this by *Andantino grazioso* rather than a "dying" *Adagio* which tradition has so far dictated. Indeed it may not be of momentous significance one way or the other which road we follow in this case, but as a general principle artistic integrity demands that we try to understand what the composer wished to say rather than follow some whim, or generally accepted tradition!

So the first conclusion we can come to is not to accept anything at face value. Start with a clean slate, physically and mentally rubbing out anything that has been added to the music for whatever reasons. Often it is not easy to find out what the composer actually wrote and intended, but it is far more interesting and creative to discover for yourself rather than rely on someone else's findings, however creative they may be.

"If you understand the structure of the music you are more than half way to solving the technical problems". These are the words of the Hungarian cellist Vilmos Palotai. Perhaps another way of saying Liszt's words, echoed by Kreisler, "Technique is of the mind".

We already know from our work on the physical aspects that we must experience the music and have it within us by pulsing and singing before attempting to commit it to our instrument. If our innate musical instincts do not let us down, the phrase will flow naturally to its cadence and on naturally to the next phrase, but some conscious knowledge of musical structure is vital if we are to be able to interpret with any degree of authority.

At first it would be better to work with the standard "classical" eight-bar phrase. For example the opening 'cello song from the second movement of Schubert's G major string quartet (D887) [see Ex 29].

Example 29

The phrase is naturally divided into half at the fourth bar cadence (F sharp, G, F sharp) and continues to flow through the next four bars into its cadence at the eighth bar. So far this is obvious, but what of the movement within each of the four bars? If the music flows naturally into the fourth and eighth bars it would be logical to assume that there is a lesser flow into the second and sixth bars. In fact the first bar flows into the second and so on from each odd-numbered bar into each even-numbered bar. It is always better perhaps to speak of "flows" rather than "accents" or "stresses" as these latter terms tend to make us think of music in sections. So a lighter first bar flows into a heavier second bar.

How many times do we automatically start on a down bow? Looking at a symmetrical eight-bar phrase it would be normally unnatural to finish on anything but a down bow on the final note. So in such a symmetrical phrase the even-numbered bars would be generally down bow and the odd numbers up bow. The first bar being an up bow would help it not to be a heavy accent and naturally flow to the stronger second bar on the down bow. Also remember that the pulse out of which the first note is born (and bourne) is riding on that endless musical flow so that the inward movement of the right arm is perhaps a more natural movement with which to connect it to the flow. Should it be necessary for a musical reason to start with a down bow any hint of accent can be avoided if the right arm is on a horizontal swing!

What we are doing is finding out what happens through understanding the structure! Already the music has guided us to the bowing to choose. The fingering of this phrase has a few possibilities but it must always be chosen in conjunction with the bowing and in the service of the music. We will take a different phrase later to highlight choice of fingering in greater detail.

Another facet brought to light in this phrase is the nature of repeated notes, which so often appear as beautifully-played martelé accented little "bumps" having no particular place or significance in the phrase. The two D sharps in bar 3 are parts of different motifs, the first one belongs to the E before the barline creating an iambic flow across. The second D sharp's function is an upbeat for the following quavers leading to the fourth bar's F sharp-G-F sharp cadence. The execution of the two D sharps with the dot and the line over them ($\bar{\cdot}$) is fractionally to shorten the first one (through the left hand) and to give the second its full legato value leading it to the quaver F sharp, thus producing a natural musical gap between them. This underlines the fact that they do not belong to the same musical motif and the same applies to the two E's in the seventh bar.

Superficially this may seem to break up the phrase, but in practice if the process is fully understood it enhances the flow. Nothing breaks up the flow more than two little repeated notes that do not belong anywhere.

Normally the climax of the phrase or piece comes two-thirds or three-quarters of the way through. This is no exception, the climax coming on the C in the sixth bar led up to by the G. It is not always necessary to let the bowing follow the iambic flow across the barlines, but in this case it works in the first part. However, at the climax, when it is desirable to have more movement and energy it may be better to change the bow direction between the upbeat G and the climax C, always remembering that the left hand leads.

It might be helpful to have a look at a rather unusual eight-bar phrase from the third movement of Beethoven's F minor quartet (Op. 95) [Ex 30].

Example 30

What is the problem? Normally one would pounce very strongly on to the motif marked forte in the first and third bars which automatically leaves "musical vacuums" in the silent second and fourth bars. Is this not what Beethoven intended? If the result is to give the impression that the silent bars are just marking time without a living dynamic pulse, then NO! On the other hand if the first bars were to be a strong forte without accent, and if the pulse was to be aimed throughout the first bar towards the extremely strong pulse in the second bar, which is silent, then the impression given would be a strong flow into the silent bar preparing for the next forte in the third and so on into the eighth bar. This demonstrates the function of rests in music as an alive part of the musical flow rather than what the name "rest" implies, just a break and marking time!

The choice of fingering is a subject which causes more confusion and dissent than any other in the string players' world. An easy way out is to say that fingering is left to personal taste. There can only be one way. Fingering is decided entirely by the way the music goes.

But which way does the music go? This is exactly what we are trying to find out. "When we understand the structure of the music we are more than half way to solving the technical problems" cannot be repeated too often, and fingering is so much part of the solution that fingering and bowing, which must be inseparable, can only be chosen by the nature of the music. So just as the composer's feelings are the ones that matter rather than one's own, so the music chooses the bowing and fingering rather than personal whim. There are many bad and unworkable fingerings (and bowings) that could be chosen, but only a few good and workable ones that will serve the music.

It seems at first that the kaleidoscopic nature of the music lends itself to so many permutable possibilities for the fingering and bowing combination that, initially, one gives up and accepts the first thing that comes to mind. It is often overwhelming to be faced with a new piece of music that has been fingered and bowed by an editor (not always a string player!) or that has not been edited at all, waiting for enlightenment so that the bowing and fingering will serve the flow of the music. It is always better to start with a clean slate as another editor's ideas, of whatever quality, would be their ideas and not your understanding of the musical structure.

Are there any universal ground rules for this subject which would help in making a start? "Change bow with change of position when musically feasible and change position on the smallest interval whenever possible (look for the semitones)" is very good advice and can help very much in eliminating bad choices. It so often happens that shifts are made from one familiar position to another just because they are familiar and have nothing to do with the musical flow. In the normal process of learning we start in the first position (first finger B on the A string) and then the fourth position (first finger E on the A string). This is probably the first true shift we ever learn and as such leaves a deep psychological scar. To move out of our home territory as a beginner into an unknown region is a shock. Here is a good example of how the "outside-in" approach is anti-music. If the intervals to be "shifted" were first known by pulsing and singing, the process would be from "inside-out" and the shift would no longer hold any terrors.

However, physically, we are delighted to discover that this new unknown fourth position (in old terminology) is quite comfortable as the thumb sits easily in the crook of the neck so this very soon becomes a second home; just like a bolt-hole! After that we do not want to know any more; we do not wish to know anything about possibilities between the first and fourth positions which become a sort of "no-go area". Music is then forced into the first and fourth positions. But music cannot be forced into any pre-arranged package if it is to stay alive!

Let us find a phrase which falls between the range of these positions so that we can discover how the flow dictates the fingering (Ex. 31).

Example 31: Arioso - Bach

Such a piece is the well-known Arioso by Bach, arranged from a harpsichord concerto, and we see that if the structure is understood, the first finger on the opening B followed by another first finger on the semitone shift, C, the first of three semiquavers leading to A, is not only desirable but inevitable. The tied crotchet B belongs to the flow before the start which is then followed by the motif C-D-E semiquavers into the tied crotchet A. This solution is not only following the ground rules of shifting on the smallest interval, the semitone, and changing bow on the change of position, but serves the music in every way. Starting the first B on an up bow helps to avoid a heavy accent at the start and then the following down bow on the semiquavers helps their forward movement as the arm opens out to the point on the last part of the swing.

Then the last semiquaver E, fourth finger, can be displaced by the third finger coming from behind forward into the A on the lower D string. The feeling of opening out into the major disposition to prepare the D and E semiquavers after the first shift B to C between the motifs should be as natural as breathing.

However, after the tied A in the middle of the bar it is better to finger the B-C-D semiquavers-first, second and third fingers on the D string, having a tone shift between A and B as this is the gap between motifs rather than shift during the slurred semiquavers on the B-C interval. In this case we take the change of the bow as preference. Obviously it does not always work out that the smallest interval and bow change coincide as they do so conveniently at the start of this piece, but there is always something one can do to serve the flow of the music.

This is extremely creative work and if you find that constructive ideas dry up then it is better to break off, have a rest and wait for ideas to start coming again. The worst possible thing is to carry on in a mechanical way using bowings and fingerings that are possible, but in no way serve the music.

Never forget the possibility of the opening and closing of the left hand, closing either to a tone or semitone shape, and opening to either a minor or major third shape mentioned in the chapter on shifts. Look at the passage in descending thirds in the second section in E minor of the Sarabande of Bach's G major suite (see Ex. 32).

Example 32

Each third, A-F sharp, G-E, F sharp-D sharp (on to E semitone) can be fingered fourth to first finger each time. But remember it is the semitone F sharp-G, the tone E-F sharp, and finally the D sharp-E, the rising steps and half steps which connect the descending thirds, which are the musically significant intervals. This must be so as it is the D sharp -E which brings the phrase to rest. Also notice prior to this passage, that to take the G with the third finger instead of the fourth, opens out the hand to the major disposition which helps to negotiate the semitone distance to the A after the F sharp

- E. From this we can feel that it is the contraction of the left hand to either tone or semitone which is sculpting the shape of the most important intervals physically, so this positive shaping is serving the music!

It depends upon the tempo of a particular passage in thirds as to which fingering is chosen. At a quicker tempo than the above example, it would not be advisable to attempt such a solution but rather a series of well chosen shifts in the normal dispositions.

Clinging to generally held, but nevertheless misplaced ideas can be responsible for strange and even bad fingering. In normal circumstances it is obvious that the first finger is stronger than the fourth. It is hoped from what we have seen in all the previous chapters that we have more than enough potential energy in the smallest digit to serve any musical need we may have for it.

A generally accepted fingering for the first interval in the Saint-Saens' A minor concerto seems to be first finger on the first tied E moving to the D of the triplets with the fourth finger. This is a comparatively large shift at the outset, but the first finger feels "at home" and "strong" in the old fourth position, and yes, this first E does belong to the opening chord on the orchestra which is part of the pre-start flow, with the following triplet flow belonging to the next motif. However, if you are confident that the entry is not instigated by any such small thing as a finger but comes from much larger physical forces in balance, then why not make life easier and start on the fourth finger on E, shift a tone to D, also with the fourth finger, and on a change of bow? This will feel strange at first if you have always done it the other way, which opens another facet in the process of choosing fingerings.

It is understandable to opt for that which is most familiar and very often we can perpetuate a fingering which does no service to the music, but we do it because we have always done it that way. This is why it is always better, when coming back to a work done many times previously in the distant past, to wipe the slate clean and look at it again as though it were for the first time. A classic case is the famous opening of the William Tell overture by Rossini.

Example 33

An obvious choice of fingering could be the lower set in Example 33. The only drawback is the last interval of the first bar, B to E, which comes under a slur, and if played by a first finger shift will produce as scoop, or a "Wah" sound, however well executed.

Initially the upper fingering will not immediately seem to be an easy solution. But once the interval shapes are second nature to the left hand you will find it serves the music admirably. After the D sharp - E semitone shift with the first finger at the start of the semi-quavers there is the E minor arpeggio in the minor disposition. The only slight problem is the true extension between the two groups of semi-quavers for the perfect fourth interval B to E with the large fan between first and fourth fingers.

After that, the next octave of the E minor arpeggio is done across the G and D strings, in the major disposition, finishing the group with a contraction to a tone shape between fourth and first finger (on the A string), which is the interval that caused the problem in the first place in the lower fingering.

Finally the hand opens to a minor third shape to the fourth finger G.

This may seem to be going to a great deal of trouble just to get rid of one little "Wah" sound, but if these disturbing unmusical shifts are perpetuated many times in a piece they become very tiresome and impinge on the music.

The variations and possibilities in the choice of bowings and fingerings are enormous and the only criterion is "Do they serve the music?" It is an exciting and creative activity finding out how to translate the music in practical terms to your instrument. If such work becomes boring or mechanical you will very soon know how unmusical the result will be.

To round off this section which is only the tip of the iceberg in a never-ending study, let us take as an example the opening phrase of Brahms' E minor sonata to bring together all the strands we have looked at so far.

Before we can make any decision regarding the 'cello part it is essential to have the overall picture from the piano score and so we will always work from that. The first impression we get is of an unusually low melodic line for the 'cello accompanied by off-beat crotchet chords on the piano which actually continue through to the climax, C, in the second phrase. It has been suggested that this sonata is a homage to J. S. Bach as this first theme is derived from Contrapunctus IV in the Art of Fugue (the last movement's main theme is even more closely related to Contapunctus XIII of the same work).

Throughout the work and particularly on this opening phrase we will be tasting and experiencing the dark "minor" drama of the intervals. The off-beat crotchets of the piano give a feeling of unrest or underlying turbulence like the iron fist in a velvet glove. This must be one of the most powerful "piano" melodic lines ever written so low on the 'cello. The fact that it came from a Bach fugue subject may not have a direct bearing, but the more we know the better will be our understanding.

In a work in sonata form it is always a good idea to compare the exposition section with the recapitulation at the start, and in this case we will find an identical 'cello line in this first phrase but the piano part is embellished by the right hand playing descending quaver figures while the left hand still has the initial off-beat chords. The fact that the harmonies are not rapidly changing allows the melodic line to flow freely and the off-beat chords suggest an overall minim pulse enhancing the forward flow. The quavers in the recapitulation in the piano part point to the inner pulse movement which is in quavers. It also indicates that this quaver movement must be crystal clear and therefore the tempo must not be over-quick.

So we first pulse and sing the intervals in quavers as in Example 34.

Example 34: Inner Pulse in Quavers

Pa Pa Pa Pa   Pa Pa Pa Pa   Pa Pa Pa Pa

This gives us the "inside-out" flow of the music and makes absolutely sure of the value of the first quaver B in the first bar as related to the G and the C and all subsequent quavers and semiquavers, including the written-out turn in bar 3 (see Example 35).

Example 35 *Allegro non troppo*

Looking at the motivic structure, we see the normal start of the first note belonging to the previous flow followed by the G-B-C-motif and so on until the F sharp- G sharp-A sharp-B ending the phrase.

In the bowing and fingering chosen, you will notice that as the bars do not contain much in the way of uniform pattern they will not conform to an up-down, up-down format; however, you will notice the E in the fourth bar is down but the B ending the phrase is up. This works well in the first phrase but it is also a good preparation for the start of the second. As the second phrase starts calmly with a down bow it will be in exactly the right place to start without a disturbing physical movement necessary had the B been on a down bow.

The first E will start higher up in the down bow as the following motif, apart from the quaver B, is all up bow and so now will be well balanced. Also by starting the first E higher in the bow it will be in the more accelerated part of the swing which will give it a clarity without an accent which this low generating note demands. It is so important that this first note is a sort of "silky generator" and of course the bow can only play "the slave" in this. It is the sponged left hand through the rounded "back edged" first finger that determines the final quality. Then the fourth finger rounds into the G on the swing of the up bow followed by the first finger articulating the quaver B coming in from behind forward on the small swing down bow (remember the Pa-Pa movement; the first right arm movement we made?). It is so important that this B quaver to the minim C is done exactly right so that you will feel the strong connection of the interval. Just a suspicion of over-reaction in the right arm will spoil the left hand's articulation, which must be strong and clear. This is exactly where the inner pulse quaver energy helps.

Although the minims C to B in the second bar are slurred they belong to different motifs and there is a choice of fingering here. If we go from the B on a first finger to the A in the next bar this gives us a change of position on a change of bow which is acceptable, but if we change position from C, second finger, to B with the same finger it is a shift on a semitone albeit not on a change of bow. If we do it this way the written-out turn in bar 3 is done with the tone interval A-B with the first and second fingers rather than the first and third fingers. The advantage of this is that the hand in the third bar is opened out to the major disposition, which means the G quaver at the end of the bar is only a semitone shift away to take it with the fourth finger on the C string, so that the answering motif to the opening B-C, G-E can be taken on the C string with the fourth and first fingers. An open G here would not be too happy.

The second half of the phrase starts with a slurred "bridge note" F sharp over the barline which is shaped from the preceding E by closing the left hand to a tone shape and then opening to a minor third shape for the D sharp., the first of the three ascending quavers. These three quavers continue as pulsed up bows from the tied F sharp. Again it is the left knuckle articulation which controls these notes and though there is a slight amount of air between each note they are very legato quavers pulsed through the left hand into the D sharp still on the G string. Notice the motivic quaver, F sharp into the same note (minim) in the next bar. Also notice that the minims F sharp octave are belonging to different motifs which makes the lower F sharp to the high G the significant interval (minor ninth) and the same again down to the low F sharp dotted crotchet. There must be a tremendous energy sent through the G sharp-A sharp semiquavers to the final B with the left hand articulation as these can get smudged so easily on the C string.

The slightly unusual use of the fourth finger on the G in the penultimate bar disturbs the shape of the left hand less than if the more usual third finger were used. The feeling is that as the octave F sharp is done between fourth and first fingers, the G is only a semitone more for the fourth to fan and back again to the low F sharp. As mentioned earlier the direction of the bow for the B is important so as not to disturb the "bridging" rest between phrases, hence it is not possible to work on a phrase in isolation, as what happens in any phrase has a bearing on the next (and also the previous one).

As far as the overall flow pattern goes this phrase is in the normal classical mould; the first bar flows into the second, the third slightly more strongly into the fourth, with the second half following the same pattern, but with a greater flow into the eighth than into the fourth. The last B is suspended hanging in mid-air on the pulse over the rest preparing the C for the new major key of the second phrase.

When we have acquired a good taste and feel for the phrase we should try to decide on a natural tempo on which the music flows easily and if indeed the tempo of the first phrase will be valid for all of the rest of the movement. Maybe this is not a piece for a uniform tempo; however let us try something like minim equals 58 or 60, making crochet equal to 116 or 120 would be a good start. This particular interpretation of the motivic structure may not be to everyone's taste, but as long as it helps to avoid heavy first - beat accents and the restriction of bar-lines, any sensible realization of the structure is preferable in order to allow the music to flow. This all being established, we are now in a position to go through all the stages of miming, first without and then with the instrument.

This is a highly concentrated work and takes many words to describe, but we take short cuts at our peril. It is possible that if one is particularly gifted in sight-reading there may not be the inclination to go into the music in such detail for fear of ruining the spontaneity. This is where talent could be a blindness, for no real creative work will get in the way of spontaneity. Once we have gone to this amount of trouble the music is ours for life. This does not mean that we shall interpret and play things the same way over a lifetime. It is hoped that we are able to grow and develop in musical understanding and make changes accordingly, but these changes will be because of better understanding and not because of a whim! Any hint of this work becoming "academic" or mechanical is death to music. If it is always creative, as it is intended to be, the interest and excitement will be self-generative, always.

Chapter 13
Practice And Performance
Practice

A jaundiced view of the old cliché "practice makes perfect" could be "the chaotic in search of the unattainable". All sorts of problems and tensions arise when we begin to strive for "perfection".

Sound advice on the subject of practice seems to be in short supply, probably because it is generally viewed, like the choice of bowing and fingering, as something very personal and therefore left to the individual. However, it is a very large and important subject and some guidelines are offered here in the hope that they will be of help.

The initial form of practice is to work on the fundamental principles in order to maintain and develop one's basic technique, and if Liszt is to be believed that "technique is of the mind" then the percentage of mental work far outweighs the practical work on the instrument. Never feel that it is a waste of time to remind yourself of the fundamental balances. Go back to the beginning - check the posture, the arm balances, put yourself in physical shape!

It is also necessary to understand at the outset that it is only possible to concentrate at the required level for a few minutes at a time, so that whatever you are working on, whether it is the basic scale intervals or a more complex study, decide on a specific short section and stick to it. *Always* pulse and sing it first, then go through the miming process - put the right arm joints in order, then control them with the left hand, shaping the intervals. Do this first away from the instrument and then with it, always pulsing and singing, *and only the section that you have chosen*. That requires discipline! It is all too easy to meander on mindlessly playing into the next section which is not yet prepared. This is always a waste of time. How many times do we think that we just don't have enough time to practice, so why waste it?

Now we can think about the music.

It is a good idea to change the order of doing things from session to session so that you never feel that you are "ploughing the same furrow" all the time. Nothing numbs the music sensibility more than mindless repetitive practice which really isn't doing anything for you except reinforcing problems and mistakes. Unless you are enjoying what you are doing, it is better not to do it, as there is no feedback.

On the other hand there is nothing more exciting than discovering something which makes it possible for you to produce music effortlessly. Surely this is always our goal in practice?

It might be a good idea to discuss here what appears to be a major stumbling block with this approach. Professional players and serious students coming to these ideas for the first time are often very resistant to singing and pulsing. As to saying the note names at the same time, that is right out! They protest that it is putting another step in an already unfamiliar process and it is very difficult to persuade them of the necessity of so doing: all of which is most understandable.

You only have to go into a high position on the A string to play notes (intervals) with which you are familiar; but then can you immediately identify which notes exactly correspond to these across on the C string which are not so familiar? In most cases you would have to be honest and answer, no.

Also, if you play the first octave of a scale on the same string you would probably know which notes you were playing and what the interval shapes were. However, if we were to carry on to the second octave on the same string, although the notes and intervals are the same, it is possible that you would not be quite as sure as you were in the first octave. So when you really need to know what note you are playing, because you need to discover the resonance to a degree, high on the instrument, this is the very time that you perhaps do not identify the notes as you should.

The name of the game is "identification" and if "sol-fa" is preferred so be it, but it behoves you to *know* what you are playing!

If you are high on the C string you will want help from the natural harmonics of C and G, and also help from the open A and D strings. Of the eight notes of the octave five of them, two C's, G, D and A all have immediate help, but if you are not clear exactly what note you are playing how can you find the full resonance? No apologies for repeating this facet again.

Would that we were all brought up to do it the Kodaly way from childhood, we would not be faced with something new and strange to overcome and our music making would be that much more exciting!

Whatever we are doing as far as the work on fundamentals is concerned, whether it be scale or arpeggio intervals, or studies, always work creatively with musical imagination remembering that out of scales and arpeggios composers construct concertos, symphonies, string quartets or whatever!

Just as a sculptor shapes a lump of rock, breathing life into it as he works, so does a composer organise and shape intervals, breathing life into them as the musical phrases are shaped and formed. This is the miracle of music.

So in our minds, when practising scales and arpeggios always shape them into imaginative musical shapes irrespective of the chosen tempo. (Slow scale practice is just as important as the faster variety, if not more so).

To plough mindlessly up and down scales in repetitive furrows is not only a waste of time but positively harmful as it dulls the musical imagination.

So, as promised in an earlier chapter, we will discuss how to organise the faster variety of scale practice.

If we set ourselves a challenge of playing a scale at a predetermined quick tempo, say in three octaves, we will probably fall flat on our face.

If we organise it in this way: -

Example 36

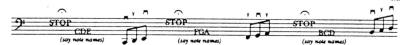

we will find that by *saying* the note names to the left hand after the rest with an immediate mime response by the left knuckles directing the fingers on the string at the same quick tempo, we will clarify our thought and teach the left hand the feeling of "sculpting" the groups of three quavers.

Follow this by actually playing the quavers *immediately* after saying the note names to the left hand. (This action is pulse-related whereas the rest is a true rest without pulse). The rest should be as long as you need at the start, and you will find that you will need a long thinking time at first to prepare the action!

When the process becomes more familiar the rests can be shortened until they can be dispensed with altogether, and then you will be just saying the note names to the left hand *immediately* followed by the played response, all on the pulse.

Finally, you will be able to connect the three quaver groups together, talking to the left hand inwardly as you surprise yourself by playing the three octaves at the desired tempo. Only aim for what is possible in not opting for too fast a tempo. Go through all the processes with patience, because if you become impatient and take short cuts you will fall on your face again!

Always remember that in this particular type of practice the extremely strong but economical, miniscule movements of the right arm from the shoulder joint in response to the left hand "sparks" is vital. During the rest the right arm and bow should *rest* in balance on the point of balance where the action will take place. As always go through the process of, first miming without the instrument *looking* at the back of the left hand to control the knuckles by saying the notes on the pulse. Next introduce the miniscule right arm movements from the shoulder joint in response.

Now do the same mime with the instrument and only then are you ready to do the exercise as suggested.

The pattern of triplets (Ex. 36) will work in three octaves and semi-quavers in groups of four in four octaves. If the higher octaves prove daunting at first it is possible to use the semi-quavers in groups of four in two octaves but the highest group will just turn the corner (in the key of C; A, B, C, B.) and down again.

Later this exercise can be used with slurs, either in opposite directions each time, or by travelling bit by bit in one direction, which is the ideal preparation for doing a number of octaves in one bow.

The well-tried practise of playing a quick passage slowly and quickening it up by degrees very rarely works up to the required tempo, or to the degree desired. But in this way of approaching the problem you are experiencing the notes (intervals) at the required tempo right away delivered in small "groups", between each "group" the body and mind has time to re-focus during the rests.

You will notice that we are only "saying" the note names on each small group. Because of the speed it would be asking a lot to sing the pitch as well. However, the inner ear will always sense the pitch as you do this.

The main object of this exercise is to connect the identification of the notes and their shape to the tactile sense in the left hand.

Always remember, the quicker the tempo, the more economical and miniscule the movements become in the left hand knuckles and right arm nudge.

For further study, see "Stage Fright" - in the chapter "The fear of not being fast enough" (pages 80-90). In fact "Stage Fright" in the words of Sir Yehudi Menuhin "is a book that should be worth its weight in gold to every student and many a performer".

As for studies, well, such masters of the instrument as Popper, Duport and others must not only have been fine instrumentalists but good composers as well as they left us a fund of good music to enjoy. A study should be, and usually is, a piece of music which is especially written to highlight and develop a particular aspect, or aspects, of technique.

It may be that there are mechanically contrived studies which are not so appealing musically, which can be avoided, making way for studies which are real pieces of music.

There are many books of "finger exercises" published, all of which may be in certain circumstances very helpful. However, these are ostensibly written to help people with stiff finger joints - the stiffness is more often in the mind! Finger exercises can be unmusical and positively dangerous if not used with understanding.

The usefulness of finger exercises is more to do with the co-ordination and synchronization of brain, tendons and muscles in fast-moving and sometimes complex note patterns (interval patterns) than the actual loosening of finger joints. For the people who really do suffer from stiff joints, the judicious use of finger exercises practised with the imaginative awareness we are talking about, will eventually help to soften the finger joints.

All scale, arpeggio and study practice should be on the same musical level as the rest of the practice and if not done with enthusiasm and joy, had better not be done at all!

The question will still be asked, "Why is it necessary to do all these scales, arpeggios and studies at all?"

To have to ask this question in the first place denotes a problem because in asking it we are ostensibly dividing in our mind scales and so on from music. It is all part of the same process. By using scales and arpeggios we are merely focusing our attention on intervals alone in a particular key organized in a formal pattern rather than having to cope all at once with a more complex variety of intervals subsequently formed by the composer.

As we have said a study is a piece of music specifically designed to enable us to focus on a particular aspect of our development. It is possible that we could achieve a stage in development when scales, arpeggios and studies could become a small part of our practice. Was it Kreisler who said that since the age of twenty he hadn't needed to do much scale practice - if any?

As long as we understand the need for fundamental exercises and never allow them to get out of proportion and rule our practice time, we will always enjoy practising them.

Perhaps one of the most difficult departments of practise to deal with mentally is that of returning to re-work a piece of music learned previously.

It is true that over a period of time a searching musician will continue to think consciously (and apparently unconsciously) about music that he has learned, and one would expect that in coming to a piece again it would be with greater maturity and understanding each time it comes around.

There is another scenario; that of being confronted with something familiar and in a desperate attempt to make it more interesting, more "musical", this time around, to change things for the sake of change. It goes without saying that this is a recipe for disaster.

Nearly all music of any worth has many layers of meaning to be uncovered and discovered, and any artist will go on until his dying day searching for what is there, so in these circumstances it is not possible to get tired of, or become bored with music, so to change anything for the sake of change is right out! The only reason for change is if we discover a better way of doing something which serves the music better.

The greatest satisfaction comes when we find a solution staring us in the face which is so simple and straightforward that it is hard to understand why we did not see it before. This is why it is a good idea to leave a work for a time in order to stand back from it, and when we do come back to it, *look at it as if it were for the first time.* This is a very important concept.

If we have understood the fundamental structure of the music in the first place, it is obvious that as that does not change, we will only have to make changes regarding the things we have missed or misunderstood in the first place. The misunderstanding could be in the way the phrase or motif is constructed, but if the particular composer's work is thoroughly understood, it is unlikely that fundamental mistakes would be made too often. It is more likely that it would be in the details that changes would take place and when these are totalled up, they could have quite a significant impact on the whole.

A small example of this happened in the opening of the Brahms' E Minor Sonata discussed earlier. As suggested, the minims C and B in the second bar could be fingered by the second and first fingers respectively or by the second finger making a semitone shift between the two minims. (This of course contravenes the dictum "change position on a change of bow whenever possible"). However, as discussed earlier, the shift on the second finger serves the music a little better as it helps the hand to open out into the major disposition which prepares what follows, (see Ex. 35). This is only a small change, but it only takes one or two of these changes to make both performer and consequently the audience, happier.

Another small example, this time what could be called a technical example, is a short passage from the beginning of the last movement of the Schumann Cello Concerto. Some commentators suggest that Schumann thought "pianistically" and his string writing therefore did not fall easily for the string player. Certainly, this last movement could be an example of this, coming as it does after two wonderfully lyrical movements.

Example 37

In the arpeggiated passage of Example 37, a fingering which could first come to mind is Ex. 37a. In the first A Minor arpeggio, the fingering of fourth finger on the low A with the first contracting to a tone shape for the octave above, followed by the C and E in the same position, is good for that arpeggio, but then there is a comparatively big move to the thumb for the next A (fourth interval shape shift) followed by an extended interval shape of a minor sixth shape to F. It might be flippant to suggest that this fingering might work if the wind was in the north-east and there was not an R in the month!

Perhaps the following might work better, having had a new look at it (Ex. 37b). As the low A on the C string motivically belongs to the previous passage, it would seem more natural to make a very slight rubato break between the octave shift, so that the following arpeggio A, C, E, A, which is a complete motif, falls naturally in the same position and then the coming interval of a minor sixth (A to F sharp) is easier to prepare, which gives the final motif of the passage, F to E. With the earlier solution, the shift from E (first finger) to A (thumb) disturbs the feeling for the coming minor sixth shape. In the later solution, the main problem is the ease of execution of the octave shift from the low A on the C string to the first finger A on the G string. When this has been achieved, the intervals that follow should fall into place more naturally. It could be that there is a better solution for this passage for another individual, but whatever the piece, never take anything for granted; always search for the best solution, certainly in this particular movement it will pay dividends.

One's attitude to this aspect of practice is very important because it is part of the key to general musical development.

The easy way out is just to accept and do what we did previously without another thought, which is a dead end, and for an artist that is unthinkable.

As we have said, if we re-work a piece as though we had never seen or heard it before, all the excitement and enthusiasm brought about by meeting a wonderful new work for the first time will be generated all over again, which brings us naturally to the last section of practice.

Probably the most exciting and fulfilling work, apart from actual performance, that one can do on (and off) the instrument is working on a new piece for the first time with which one has an affinity. It is almost as creative work as composition itself, because you are taking the music and translating it for, and to, the 'cello.

We have gone through all the suggested stages with specific examples in the chapter on Interpretation, so there is no point in repeating similar examples here.

It has been suggested that a format for practice of a new piece could be to look at it to find all the "difficult" bits, which you would then "take out" separately and practice them like mad, leaving the "easy" sections to look after themselves. This is a sort of "quick study" syndrome, brought about by the great malaise of our age - shortage of time!.. Again, this is a recipe for disaster. Just try it and you will fervently wish, in performance, that you had made time for the "easy" bits.

If music is prepared properly, both mentally and physically, there should be no question of there being "difficult" or "easy" bits - there is just music. That is not to say that there is not more "complicated" music or more"simple" music, but that is another question.

Let us study an example of how to approach quick-moving passages, which can so often be unclear, at best, and "garbled" at worst.

The opening of the second movement (Allegro) of Vivaldi's E Minor Sonata would be a good example (Ex. 38).

Example 38

We have here a mixture of note values - quavers and semi-quavers - grouped in a specific way and unless we discover the structure of this arrangement we cannot progress.

For now, ignore the up beat quaver B and practice the groups of four semiquavers as we did in the "fast" scale practice (see Ex. 36). Rest -say E, G, F, E - immediately play E, G, F, E. (F in this case means F sharp - there isn't time to say the "sharp", so just think it). Then after a rest say B, G, F, E, and immediately play it. Not wanting to make a competition out of it, choose a tempo of something under crotchet = 100. Don't forget to mime the semi-quavers prior to actually playing them - i.e. rest, say E, G, F, E, immediately mime E, G, F, E. Watch the back of the left hand as the knuckles articulate these intervals. At first you will find that you will have to do this at a fairly slow tempo!

We have now accounted for the two groups of semi-quavers.

However, there are still problems. If we now put these two groups together - E, G, F, E, - B, G, F, E - without a break, the fifth E to B is troublesome as the B can so often "cough" or miss out slightly due to the problem of how to get from the E with the first finger.

If the strings are reasonably close together we can solve the problem by using the north- west side of the D string and the north - east side of the A string as the first finger sits comfortably between, which is good. *Always remember to send the pulse from the first finger knuckle through to the contact on the B!*

What about the quavers on either side of these two semi-quaver groups?

To answer that we will have to look at the motivic structure (see Ex. 38). From this you will see the semi-quaver groups are now - rest - say G, F, E, B, mime and play them - rest - say G, F, E, B, mime and play them.

The last note of the second group is one of the two quavers. The first motif is B - E making the up beat quaver swing over the barline into the semi-quaver E. This interval has tremendously strong "glue" between it and needs a very strong and economical nudge from the right arm in response to the left hand's third and first knuckle. Work the B - E interval in both directions, B -E - E - B, and also try both "up - down" and "down - up" with the bow.

Incidentally, change the bow directions like this when doing the four semi-quavers in both groupings.

We have now organised the first three motifs. Now if the first B - E has "glue" between it, the C - B of the fourth motif has "superglue". The clarity of articulation of this interval is central to the success of the whole first phrase.

As we have tried opposite directions of the bow, which one is preferable? Without question, the one quoted in the example is the stronger as the last note of the third motif, B, comes on an up bow to come "down" on the vital C in the right arm's natural swing.

Although this means that the first quaver, B, upbeat comes on the less usual down bow and the semi-quaver groups start with an up bow, it seems to work throughout the phrase this way, particularly as we said on the big B - C interval on the third main crotchet pulse.

Do not take anything for granted - try it the other way! Although this approach is put forward as the better way of achieving clarity in quick passages, this does not mean that the initial familiarisation with the intervals of a quick-moving piece should not be done at a slow tempo, in fact it is essential that at first it should be realised at a very moderate and very accomodating tempo; it is just that by quickening up by degrees you will eventually reach the tempo at which the passage didn't work for you before - and it still doesn't!'

It is hoped that what we have discussed here, and in the previous section about scales will endorse the words of Kató Havas "there is no such thing as fast playing".

If you work properly from "inside out" phrase by phrase, and if it is a large work, in sections sometimes starting with the last section working backwards to ensure each section receives the same attention, time will not exist for you. It will actually take up a lot of time, but working creatively, you will never have to spend this amount of time on this particular piece again.

Obviously, there will be places when you will come up against a blank wall. What should happen here? Remember what we said about concentration levels earlier - you can only concentrate at the required level for short periods of time. When you come to an impasse, don't just do something for the sake of getting past it, which will probably be just mechanical and hence unmusical, put the problem on the "back burner" for a while, let it simmer, then later you will probably come across a solution that, as we found in the previous section, is so simple we cannot understand why we hadn't seen it before.

The whole essence of this work is not that you or I are finding ways of playing a particular piece, but that we are trying to discover how the music can flow through the 'cello without interference and only when we have done this are we ready to play.

Performance

The moment of truth has arrived - all we have done, all we have worked for and thought about, has now to be "given".

How many of us have wondered why it is that, after all that careful work and preparation, when we come to perform the passages we thought we knew so well, they seem to fall apart - our fingers feel like sausages - and in those lovely long legato passages, which we did so easily in practice, the bow judders like a machine-gun?

Unless we have been extremely lucky, these feelings must have been experienced by some of us at some time or other.

Why do they happen?

"Stage Fright" is the scourge of most performing artists, and for the string player, (violinists and violists) the subject has been dealt with in unique fashion in a book of the same name by Kató Havas, consequently it is a "must" for anyone who suffers from it, and by it.

Before we discuss the mental approach and aspects of performance, which is of course the crux of the matter, there are practical and commonsense details to be considered which can be so often overlooked.

Much good advice has been given about preparing for performance, such as what not to eat or drink and so on. Carl Flesch's advice that it is not sensible to eat too much or drink stimulants, like tea or coffee, before a concert, is good.

Generally, common sense should prevail, however there can be a danger here of generating compulsions and taboos - if I don't eat or drink such and such or if I don't do certain things before a concert I won't be able to play.

It is best to keep as near to one's normal way of life as possible, which is often difficult when coping with transport problems (particularly significant for 'cellists) with lack of facilities and such things as pianos out of tune or at the wrong pitch - the list is endless!

It goes without saying that the two main practical facets, which are a "must" for the 'cellist's comfort and peace of mind, are a chair or stool of the correct height and a secure place to fix the end pin. One good idea is to take with you your own adjustable piano stool if possible, or if not a couple of small boards which could be put across the seat of a chair to build up its height.

Such things as making sure that the bow does not go too long without being re-haired and not over "resining" it, will help.

So we can assume the practical details have been taken care of.

It could be, if we liken our practice and preparation to a well-organised pack of playing cards, that in performance it is as if we throw the pack high into the air in the hope that they fall in some sort of order.

How do we see to it that this can't happen?

Our first mental picture, after settling down on the platform , is to throw "a circle of silence" round ourselves (and our audience). How often do we start too soon without enough mental preparation?

What now?

If ever we need our "inner voice", our "inner pulse", we need it now!

As the sign of the cross is said to banish Dracula, so does the "inner pulse song" banish stage fright and nerves!

After we create our "circle of silence" we sing inwardly, pulsing the first few bars to ourselves before starting.

Could it be that for those who have not really experienced stage fright to any degree, and apparently there are a few, they have always had, within themselves naturally, a very strong "inner pulse song"?

For those of us who are not so blessed, we have to develop, to nurture this "inner pulse song" all the time, and the time we most need it is in performance. This is what prevents us throwing the cards in the air. In fact we should be so taken over by the "inner pulse song" that *we become the music.*

It can never be taken as of right, that because we have worked as hard and as long as it is possible to work in practice, the end-result in performance will happen automatically. It won't, we have to regenerate everything one hundred per cent in the here and now.

The last thing to do is to try to fight stage fright head on - it will still be there like the great negative thing it is. By using positive things - the music itself riding on the pulse - the tremendous "inner voice" - there will be no room for our ego or the negative stage fright.

How many times does one hear "I'm shaking all over before I start, but when I get going I'm all right"?

As a practical example, the present writer's "horror" was always the opening of the second movement of Beethoven's Op.95 quartet, which starts with the 'cello alone on a descending scale (see Ex. 39).

Example 39

It would be difficult to describe the agony of knowing that in performance the bow would be likely to "judder" like a machine-gun on that last minim A. Once the "inner pulse" was introduced - D um - C sharp - um - B - um - A - um - G - um - Fsharp - G sharp - A - A - A -A....., the pulsing quavers through the A in the left hand motivates the right arm, and consequently the bow, into a swinging pulsing arc that is unable to judder!

The rest - um - is as strong a pulse as the note and controls the exact length of the rest through the left hand. It is also the rest - um - which is connected to and prepares the next note coming (see Appendix - study no.2).

Also notice how the pulses on the last minim A make it possible to hand over to the rest of the quartet quite naturally without any suggestion of a hiatus.

So it can be said in practice that the "inner pulse song" not only banishes the effect of stage fright, but solves many other problems there may be as well.

All the fears of "Am I loud enough?", "Can I play fast enough?", "Will I be in tune?" and so on, (see Stage Fright) will evaporate in the wake of the pulse.

Never try to force the music across to your audience, or to adjust to a particular acoustic, or be put off by what you feel to be a poor acoustic. Always do what you normally do, because if you try to force the music through, because you feel you are not going to reach the audience at the back, you will destroy the very thing that you are trying to do. The natural energy flow will ensure that everyone is included in the music.

As Isaac Stern so graphically explained when recounting his adventure in Israel during a Scud attack warning: "Try to bring the audience to you. Create a stillness out of which Bach demands that you will listen to him".

When listening to the great interpreters, like the Hungarian Quartet or the conductor Karl Böhm, it is as if they take you by the hand to lead you clearly and simply through the music to its inevitable close. It would be difficult to visualise it done any other way!

It would also seem proper to end with a quotation from the end of Kató Havas' video. "You will always sing from inside to the left hand, and the left hand will activate the right arm". If you understand how to do this to the required degree, you will be able to give joy to others......

As she says finally: "I wish you joy in your playing, and I wish you joy in giving joy to others".

Appendix

This section is based on the "Études du Jeune Violoncelliste" by Feuillard (published by *Edition Delrieu*, Nice, France) and as it is not possible to reproduce the whole of the first twelve studies discussed here it will be necessary to have a copy. There are 60 short studies in this volume and apart from the higher thumb position studies and the larger shifts, all the fundamental basic technique is encapsulated in these first twelve studies.

All the subsequent studies will prove very useful if approached in the same light as these first twelve, also the eight volumes of "La Technique" studies by Feuillard are some of the best works in this genre in the 'cello literature. All the best 'cellist-composers are included in a sensibly graded set of studies right through all eight books.

Most of the fundamental principles, for which the first twelve studies from "Études du Jeune Violoncelliste" have been used, are treated in the main text, but for the sake of the completeness of this appendix everything will be explained in detail again, with the page reference of where the particular point appeared in the main text.

It goes without saying, that in all this work on these studies, they should all be prepared in the usual way by clapping (pulsing), singing (the intervals) and miming.

STUDY no. 1 is purely for left hand articulation - the articulation of the base joints (knuckles).

Study no. 1

With a swinging response, release the second finger C as the first finger comes in from behind forward to articulate the B, (remember the analogy of skating) similarly for all subsequent intervals. Obviously this will only be possible at a slower tempo; when it is quickened or when it goes into the semi-quaver variant the feel of the swing between the intervals will have been established even though perhaps there isn't enough time to allow the lower finger to be released completely. Even when it gets to to the speed of a trill the lower finger should always feel "sponged" with help from the thumb, rather than "clamped".

At first it would be advisable to use separate small swinging bows at the point of balance on each quaver, after which, group the quavers in four to a bow and finally, as written in eight to a bow, under the slur.

Notice that the musical effect is not: - CB - CB etc, but C - BC - BC - BC - B | C etc.. This will be fully recognised when we come to the last two bars when the flow must be: - F - GF - GF - GF - G | C; the final quaver G leading over the barline to rest on the last long C.

Imagine that this is an accompaniment to a wonderful melodic line rather than a finger exercise!

Don't forget the "variantes".

STUDY No. 2 is used for the study of Détaché and Martelé which we looked at in the chapter on Staccato.

First of all, after learning the intervals away from the instrument, play the study using legato crotchets at the suggested tempo of crotchet = 60 in the middle by balance area of the bow. The length of bow, amount of arm swing, is dictated by the tempo.

Now try the study in the Détaché mode, which is still legato crotchets but this time done from the "mirror image" point of balance to the point of the bow - the section where the elbow joint swings out in a follow-through movement in the down bow, followed by the little backward and behind fold from the shoulder joint and fold of elbow joint to initiate the up bow.

Next comes the Martelé which uses exactly the same part of the bow as Détaché, but this time the notes become quavers followed by quaver rests, (♪ ↑) and later as per "execution". (♪↑ ↑)

Study no. 2 (A)

See the section on Staccato and make sure the sounds are "bell-like" and full of overtones. Avoid the natural tendency to hurry!

Another use for this study could be to start a short down bow at the extreme heel of the bow, as per "execution", (♪↑ ↑) allowing the right arm to "fly" the bow to the extreme point during the rests, for an up bow on the next note, to fly back to the heel. Finally try the study again, changing the direction of the bow to an up bow at the heel and a down bow at the point!

The effect is a sort of bowed pizzicato which helps to develop a great degree of control in the right arm in response to the left hand action.

It is advisable to start this exercise on the open strings first, in order to organise the right arm actions:-

Study no. 2 (B) Execute as: ♪ ↑ ↑

Heel Point etc.   For the organisation of the right arm actions.

always remembering that that in a "bowing" study such as this, it is the left hand that is really in charge on the pulse!

STUDIES No. 3 and No. 6.

In both these studies the direction in the book says "study for the right *wrist* on two strings".

As we have found it is the whole arm, in balance, working from the shoulder joint which is responsible for string crossing. Any wrist movement there may be is just a follow-through activity, but there certainly should not be any localised motivation from the wrist as there can never be any true control from such movement! So for "wrist" read "arm".

It would be a good idea to pre-empt study No. 12 and prepare these two studies through the left hand by a double-stop exercise (see chapter on double-stops).

Study no. 3

Start study No. 3 by taking the open C on an up bow bringing in the open G together with it on the down bow, then up bow D (first finger) bringing it together with the G on the down bow again.

In the third bar the same pattern continues, up bow E (third finger) then E - C (fourth finger) together on the down bow and so on until the second half of the tenth bar (B - F). This is the other main type of double stop.

Play the F first (second finger) and then the B (third finger) separately in a slurred up bow bringing them together on the down bow so that the right arm senses the lower string before the two notes are brought together.

The same pattern follows in study No. 6 where the change of type occurs in the second half of bar 3 (C - F sharp)

Study no. 6

These preparatory exercises discover the interval shapes for the left hand, which as we have said, controls the right arm movements.

First practice the string crossings in separate quavers and only then introduce the slurs.

It will be noticed how positive the right arm movment has to be, particularly at the start of study No. 3, which is on the lower pair of strings, so that the two higher Gs do not "miss" or "cough".

As in study No. 1, remember that the interval between the second and third quavers is significant, which again if we look at each of the penultimate bars, it is the eighth quaver which leads over the barline to the last note.

Study No. 6 is a good preparation for the Prelude of Bach's G major unaccompanied Suite, which is a cue for a practical summary of all we have been thinking about.

The first four bars of this prelude seem to pose more problems for the 'cellist than almost any other music in the repertoire. Why should an apparently simple progression of broken chords on the most normal harmonic progression in music, (I IV V I) all in the first position of the 'cello cause such trouble?

Why does it sound so often, uneven, unmusical and mechanical? There are many ways of bowing these first four bars, the most straightforward of which is to take eight semiquavers to the bow. Palotai's realization was to slur the first three notes, the fourth with a separate bow and the next four under a slur. A good reason for this is that in the first bar, the A is the discord in the G major chord so that the "up-down" feeling in the right arm brings out naturally the A : B motif directed through the left hand. The A : B is of course "down-up" in the second half of the bar

Example 40

(aim for ♩ 66)

It is up to individual taste which approach is chosen, but unless the left hand is totally in control it would be advisable to choose the eight semiquavers to the bow. Palotai's realization is initially more demanding, but if successfully executed, musically more rewarding! Whichever way we choose it can *still* sound "lumpy" or mechanical, and it is only when we understand the true musical nature of the phrase and motifs that we can overcome the "plodding".

The tonic pedal appears, subtly obsessive, twice in each bar, going to the final one in the fifth. Notice in the fourth bar how the left hand has to "sponge " and release with the thumb underneath to sculpt the minor third shape B to G and finally to the tone shape B to the all-important F sharp which breaks the pattern of the mould for the first time into the last pedal G. This bar needs great attention!

The flow (see Example 40) is D B A B D B D G and so on to the ninth open G. The unquoted first G belongs to the silent flow before!

Whichever way you choose to bow it, if you "think" it this way it will produce the magic of the music breaking free from the imprisoning bar lines in which the pedal Gs seem to be starting something instead of having a musical flow running into them.

This is a practical example of Kreisler's "like firing at a target", Palotai's "when you understand the structure of the music you are more than half way to solving the technical problems" and Liszt's "technique is of the mind".

An intelligent study of the "Variantes" in Studies nos. 3 and 6 will pay dividends.

STUDY No. 4 is a combination of the foregoing; that is a left hand articulation study coupled with string crossings appearing naturally in a scalic or arpeggiated progression. As before, it would be better to do it first without any slurs in order to allow the left hand to find the intervals comfortably. It would not be a good idea to go straight from single notes to six to a bow as this creates a sort of competition to see how many notes we can get in a bow. Try two to a bow, and then three before trying six. If the left hand really "knows" the intervals there will be no difficulty in playing six notes to a bow, even at a moderately slow tempo, which should be the aim at first.

Study no. 4

The first crossing F to G is brought about by the fourth finger springing off (recoiling) the C string, commanding the bow to find the G string level. It is a very positive movement, otherwise the G will "cough". This is true of all the crossings in this study in both directions and every other crossing you will ever meet in any music! However, when the crossing is from the open G to F on the C string, the lead of the fourth finger coming in from behind forward is naturally more positive than the opposite way round, so that is why the first crossing between the F and open G in the first bar needs a very strong reaction, first in the recoil of the fourth finger matched by a similar strength of reaction from the right arm.

Notice that the first bar starts on an up bow. Not only does this make it possible to follow through to finish on a down bow on the last bar, but it helps to avoid a "bump" that a heavy down bow might produce at the start. The "up - down" flow of the right arm follows the natural flow of the music through to the end.

STUDY No. 5 is quite complex, so we will leave it to the end.

STUDY No. 7 is a study for the major disposition of the left hand (see chapter on Major Disposition).

As always, train the left hand to sculpt the intervals by using separate quavers, only putting the slurs back by degrees when the left hand is ready. *Unless the left hand is one hundred per cent sure of what is required, large lengths of bow are completely wasted, even by the most momentary hesitation of the left hand.*

At the initial slow tempo always release the lower finger of the major third (D to F sharp) always only having one finger in connection with the string at any one time, which will help to ensure there is no tension.

Like the first study, imagine that this is an accompaniment to a wonderful melodic line and notice the colourful key changes in the middle. Some double-stop practice would be useful between such intervals as the D to G sharp in bars 14 and 15.

Study no.7 : first 2 bars

Study no. 7 : bars 14 & 15

STUDY No. 8. As in studies 3 and 6 for "wrist" read "arm".

First pulse, sing and mime the intervals changing each of the two quaver notes into legato crotchets, then play a section, like this in crotchets at the middle by balance of the bow making sure it is the the upper arm from the shoulder socket which controls the operation through the left hand.

Notice how small the arm movements are (see chapter on the Bow Stroke).

Now play the first few bars of the study as written but without the staccato dots, i.e. legato, keeping the quaver Pa-Pa's very strongly in contact with the string. "Winch" up the level of the whole arm a fraction, so that the bow-hair only makes contact with the lower part of the small arcs the bow is describing and you will have the required staccato effect which the dots represent.

Try this feeling on the relevant open strings first, never consciously "lifting" the bow off the string. The 'cellist probably uses this mode of bowing more than any other one type, because it is the bowing used for most accompanying passages, particularly in chamber music.

In this study, notice it is only the first few bars which are scalic, so the fingering suggested is perhaps better than having the crossing from an open A to G in the first bar.

To feel the shape of A - G - F (me - re - do) under the shape of a major disposition is good. The use of open strings in the following arpeggiated passages is also good.

[ex study 8[

Study no. 8

STUDY No. 9 is the alternate use of legato and staccato. Although it says "Study for the bow" in the original, if ever you needed control through the left hand you need it now.

After the usual preparation, pulsing, and so on, find out what the right arm does on the relevant open strings. To control this type of motif (⌣ ⌐) it will all have to be done in the middle by balance of the bow if the quavers are to sound exactly as they did in study No. 8. If the study is done as suggested at alternate ends of the bow it will have to be done so that the martelé type of staccato at the point is matched by a similar sound at the heel. This of course is possible and is an alternative to the one we are discussing here which will work better at an Allegro tempo, whereas the "heel" to "point" version using the whole bow would only work at a more stately pace.

Study no. 9: opening bars

Notice that the first legato crotchet is on an up bow and the next crotchet on the third pulse is on a down bow as it is on the third pulse that the piece finally comes to rest.

Play the first full motif (D - F - B flat) starting it in exactly the same way you did in study No. 8, but the thing is when you come to make the D and F quavers staccato (first playing them legato), it is the left hand curling with the first finger into the B flat crotchet which demands legato from the right arm.

Now start with the lower B flat with the same feeling as though there were two staccato quavers before it. Once you feel the motifs going in both directions of the arm (⌣ ⌣ ⌣ ⌣) with the left hand controlling the right arm, the study will play itself as long as the left hand "knows" the interval shapes.

Notice the fingering from bar 9 in the half position,

Study no 9: bars 9-11

the changing fifth is better done between the third finger quaver F to the second finger quaver B flat so that the second finger can rock across for the legato crotchet F, rather than having to do this between the two quavers (Bar 10).

Don't take anything on trust! Try it the other way to verify the feeling.

The upper arm is really very strong and positive in this study and "cuts" across the strings feeling the change of levels very strongly.

STUDY No. 10 was treated in some detail in the section on dotted rhythms, but for the sake of completeness we will discuss it again here.

The "execution" is one of the few places in our literature where the interpretation of (♩ ♪ ♩ ♪ | ♩) is exact.

The two dots cancel out, with the dot after the crotchet becoming a rest, and the dot over the quaver disappearing to leave a very strong and clear legato note: -

The trouble lies in the fact that the eyes see (♩ ♪) as a group, whereas the ear should hear (♪♩).

Like study No. 9 we start on an up bow as it is on the third pulse of the bar we finish, which is more natural on a down bow.

So we have a very strong two-pulse B up bow (we are pulsing in quavers) followed by a rest - um - then an equally strong, if not stronger, legato quaver F sharp to bring in its motivic partner, the high B on the A string with the first finger. The motif is F sharp - B , second finger to first finger major disposition.

What has to be understood is that the quaver into the next crotchet (followed by a rest) is a very strong legato musical unit. The "up- down" - "down-up" movement is a very strong balanced movement with comparatively small arm movements. Notice how small and strong the movement of the right arm is for the quaver. The great danger is to over-react with the right arm for the short notes producing an unwanted "skidding bump".

It is probably a good idea to make the changing fifth between the first note B and the following quaver F sharp as this opens the hand to the major disposition, which can be maintained to take the C sharp (fourth finger) in the third bar at which time the first finger can close to a minor third shape for the A sharp.

Always remember the first B belongs to what comes before and that the first motif is F sharp to B. The truth of this is confirmed if you look at the penultimate and last bars.

Study no. 10: opening bars

Study no. 10: last two bars.

STUDY No. 11 was also mentioned in the section on Dotted Rhythms.

The first thing to do is to realise the motivic structure of this Siciliano rhythm which is : -

In other words, the motivic structure comes on pulses 2, 3, 4, and 5, 6, 1. This being so, it would be better to learn the intervals through the left hand in equal quavers taking out the dotted rhythms, i.e.

When the left hand "knows" exactly what the intervals feel like, the siciliano rhythm can be re-introduced, but always do it in the motivic shape, i.e.

The first note F sharp belongs to what comes before, and as in the previous study, the same applies as far as the execution of a short note followed by a longer one in all cases.

If it is done like this, the inevitable "bounce" of this rhythm will happen quite naturally (PA - POM-POM).

Notice in the suggested fingering that all the motifs fall in the same position (or nearly so) whenever posible. The motif which ends the second bar and starts the third (G - E - A) requies a true extension of a perfect fourth shape (E - A) so the first finger fans out towards the A (fourth finger) and is released, allowing the fourth finger to alight on the A.

The dot over the first full quaver of the motif (third quaver pulse of the bar) creates the *tiniest* break between the two full quavers. In fact it is the first of these two quavers, after the semi-quaver, which is shortened by the left hand fractionally and the second quaver is a full strong legato one. This is very subtle and is done entirely under the control of the left hand. If the right arm (and bow) takes on a life of its own the strength of the "bounce" in this rhythm will be lost.

As before, in all similar motifs, the right arm movements are very small but very strong and telling, particularly in the Allegro variant. Even at Andantino it would be doubtful that the movements in the right arm could be over the full length of the bow as suggested in the original directions.

Study no. 11

STUDY No. 12 The method of approaching double stops has been treated in great detail in the relevant chapter but it will do no harm to be reminded of it again here.

There are two main types of double stop, i.e one is where the lower finger is on the lower string as in sixths, and the other is where the lower finger is on the higher string, as in thirds. The two categories appear in the first bar.

As a preparatory exercise play the E on the C string with the third finger with an up bow and bring in the C on the G string with the fourth finger to sound with it on the down bow.

Feel the soft semitone shape with the thumb softening from underneath, helping the fourth finger to "tune in" the C searching for the overtones.

This is the better direction for the right arm, feeling the lower level on the up bow and then finding the level of the two strings together in a shallow arc on the down bow.

Because of this right arm feeling, it is a good idea to achieve the inversion of this first double stop (E - C), which is now the third (C - E) slightly differently, because it is always better for the left hand to work from its natural strength, i.e. the first finger, which is now on the higher string. If we play E, first finger on the D string, this time keeping it connected with the string, over to C, fourth finger on the G string as separate notes slurred in an up bow, we arrive with the right arm on the lower string (G). We can now swing into the two notes together on the down bow for the third interval (C - E), which allows the right arm to feel as it did with the sixth interval.

The third interval just takes a little more work, but it is well worth it as so much tension can be generated from a progression of thirds if the softness of the left hand is not sought for. If the first finger takes the responsibility and the fourth is just a "guest" the tension over the back of the hand should disappear. If the hand is small and the 'cello large it is likely that the hand will have to open out quite a way towards a major disposition even for this "minor" shape.

All double stops fall into one or other category. Treat fifths and octaves like sixths.

In the second part of the study, where the crotchet movement starts, still divide each double stop, i.e E - C: E - G: E - C: G - E etc., as below before attempting to play what is written.

Never struggle with double stops - if it won't work, have a rest and start again with the lower finger, making sure that it is comfortable and always look for the soft "piano" quality at first. When it has to be forte, send more energy through, but never "fight" as you will get lost between two notes never knowing which one is causing the problem.

It would be most beneficial to practice each part separately as a single line, as we tend to forget when practising each double stop separately that they are actually both part of a horizontal flow.

After working on the lower and upper parts separately, play them again, but this time finger the note you are not playing. You will then be ready to play the study as written in a horizontal flow.

Study no. 12: opening bars
Lento

Study no.12 : bars 13-14

STUDY No. 5 is perhaps the most complex study of the group and therefore needs special attention.

For a start it is the only one in triple time which brings its own special problems.

If you will remember, when we divided up the bow in various pulses it was surprising that in triple time, pulses one and two were to the middle by balance (a comparatively short distance) but the single third pulse was from the middle by balance to the point (a comparatively long distance).

On the up bow the opposite was true; from point to "mirror" point of balance (short distance) for pulse one and two followed by the big swing to the heel for pulse three (big distance).

So if we start this study in the area of the "mirror" point of balance with a strong swing out to the point (←) on the first forte G we can swing back to the "mirror" point of balance on the D and B on the slurred up bow, followed by another up bow on the G in the second bar from the "mirror" point of balance to the heel. This could be termed "a simulated change of bow" that is, carrying on in the same direction as the previous note or notes, but giving the same effect as a change of bow. As will be seen, this effect is actually a slight break dictated by the left hand as it happens to divide the motifs in this case. The first finger B is brought to a close slightly short of its full length with the right arm responding and then the right arm can swing on from the "mirror" point of balance to the heel, giving the crotchet G its full value. The process is then reversed working to the true point of balance on the slurred down bow E - C and outwards to the point on the third open G of the study. (If there is any doubt about the definition of "mirror" point of balance look back to the section on the bow).

It is interesting to note that in this study the first few bar lines give the correct musical message to the eyes; the reason for this is that the motifs appear, rather unusually, within each bar: it is as though the bar line has been shifted one crotchet pulse to the left. This is only true for the first four bars, as two little duple motifs appear together in bars 4 and 5 which changes gear to give us the more usual 3 - 1 - 2 pulse motif to follow.

This all looks rather complicated when written down, but when you come to do it in this way the problems tend to dissolve and it will become musically simple.

Another aspect of this study is the use of the "changing fifth" to enhance certain legato aspects.

In bar 5 the slur G to D needs to be legato, and so does the interval D to G across the bar line on the change of bow from the previous bar. If we change over the barline from the previous D on the fourth finger to the third on the G, we can then take the next D (second note of the slur) on the second finger. So we have two intervals, D to G and G to D done with two changing fifths semitone shape shifts.

It is ideal to play the last note in bar 5 (the G) also with the same second finger as the previous D, because this D is very slightly shortened as described earlier, which allows time for the second finger to be "rocked" across to start the next motif. In this particular place it serves the nature of the music to play a fifth interval with the same finger!

Study no. 5

Study no. 5 : bar 5

The second line follows a similar pattern.

The third line can proceed with normal opposite direction bowing (V ∧ V ∧) because the minims and crotchets are alternated in their position in each bar so that the distance covered by the bow balances out.

The fourth line is like the first two. However, notice that the crotchet C in the fourth bar from the end needs to carry on in the down bow direction, after the previous cadential F, in order to finish the section on a down bow, which will put us in exactly the right position in the bow to do the Da Capo (𝄋).

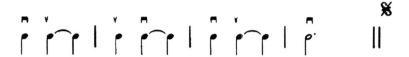

It would be so easy to destroy the music in a piece like this by "out of control" right arm movements which would create bumps and unwanted accents everywhere.

For the sake of having a look at a study for change of position and shifts we could spill over our allotted 12 studies, and at the risk of upsetting the superstitious, have a short look and comment on STUDY No. 13.

It says in the description "Study for the change of place of the left hand (first and fourth positions)".

A "position" denotes a specific place on the fingerboard for the left hand to operate and as far as music is concerned has no function whatsoever.

The whole operation should be geared to discovering which fingering (and bowing) best serves the music.

Hardly any music, because of its kaleidoscopic nature, will fit into fixed positions. Naturally, if by coincidence the music falls into certain positions, that is fine.

For instance, there was a fashion at the turn of the nineteenth century to play some of Bach's string music in the higher positions to get away from the use of open strings.

Bach wrote this music in certain keys specifically to use the sonority the open strings provide, hence the natural use of the first and lower positions was what he had in mind. However, in this study we are going to look at, this is not the problem.

If we were to accept the fact that we could only use the first and fourth positions, we would have some difficult problems.

In the first bar it would be possible to start in the fourth position (C E), fourth to first fingers, but in the second half the suggestion is to come down from the G from the fourth finger to C, second finger on the same string. This produces a rather unmusical shift with the added disadvantage of not being on a change of bow. Presumably, in the next bar, we have to swoop up again under a slur from B to G. Quite a move!

This could be all right as a position shifting exercise, but not much music will be produced; surely we could have both?

The following could be a solution:-

Study no. 13

Obviously this is not the only possibility, but if we accept the two crotchets to a bow phrasing, smaller changing fifth moves are musically more acceptable than large shifts under the slurs, which, however well done, become irritating after the first one or two. The real trick is knowing exactly when a big move is required and when it is not. Only experience and the music will tell you.

Carry on in the suggested mode to find the musical fingering for the rest of the study, that is if you have the complete study book.

The question could be asked (and probably will be) why go to all this trouble, particularly for little studies like these?

The studies provide a short musical formula, a "nursery" for music, if you like.

Think how long it would take to work on an exposition section of a Beethoven or Brahms sonata in the same way. It takes a long time! But you only have to do it once at this level and it is the most exciting and rewarding work that you can possibly do. If the composer has given his "all" to produce this music, surely the mental effort we make can never be too great.

By absorbing the principles of the "New Approach" we are given the possibility of putting this understanding of the structure of music into practice.

It may be that you have been given the great gift for music and for playing an instrument, but that is like the colour of your hair or your eyes. It is what you do with that gift that matters.

You will no doubt give a great number of people much pleasure through your playing, even if you just ride your talent, but as the Hungarian 'cellist Vilmos Palotai said "There is more to it than that." Indeed there is.!

INDEX

accent 119
acciaccaturas 98
accompanying quavers 27,
156
acoustic 147
adagio 117, 118
andantino grazioso 117, 118
anxiety 79
appoggiaturas 80, 98
arpeggios 64, 83, 86
Art of Fugue 127
articulation 44
artificial harmonics 92, 93
Associated Board of the Royal
Schools of Music v

Bach, J. S., music of 94, 127,
165,
Arioso 123
Prelude, G major suite
152
Sarabande 81, 124
Baker, Leonard iv
balance, middle by 23 et seq,
30, 32
balance of chords 69
balanced platform 8, 57, 59
balanced posture 13, 26 et
seq.
balances 8, 26, 77
Bartók, Béla 34, 115
basics 48
Bekefi, George 53
Berlin Philharmonika ii
Beethoven, L. van, music of
115, 166
Op. 70 no 1 (Ghost Trio)
iii

Op. 95 quartet 121,146
big moves 64
Boccherini, L., music of
Minuet 95
Rondo 107, 109
Böhm. Karl 147
bow connection 16, 17
bow grip 19
bow stroke 23
Brahms, J., music of 166
E minor sonata 127,128,
138
Budapest Academy iii

cadence 102
Carnegie Hall 1
Carnival of the Animals see
Saint-Saëns, C., music of
Casals, P. ii, 20
chamber music 87
change of position 53 et seq.
changing fifths 57, 60, 72,
103, 118, 157, 158, 164
chords 79, 80, 81
chromatic scale 85
choosing bowings 112, 119,
120, 122, 126, 128, 129
choosing fingerings 112, 121,
122, 123, 125,126, 129
clapping (see also pulsing) 7,
132, 133
coil and recoil 97, 154
comma, the 86
connection 5, 9, 16, 17, 72
contraction and expansion
61, 62, 124
conducting 44, 105
co-ordinated whole 6, 113
corns 59
cradle 10

slurred bowing 65, 103
sol-fah 133, 134
sonority 18, 34, **37** et seq.
spiccato 25, **105**, 107, 109
sponge **37**, 78, 100 et seq.
sponging 38, **43**, 60, 70, 89
staccato **104**, 150
Stage Fright by K. Havas 3,
    58, 136, 144, 146
Stern, Isaac 147
stopped note 69, 94
string crossing **23**, 24, 44-45,
    61, 104
Studies for Young 'Cellists
    93, 148
suspended arms **8**-10 et seq.
swing-swang 27, 113
Szekely, Zoltan ii

tactile awareness 37
tempered tuning 86, 87
tension 73, 75-76, 101 et seq.,
    161
thenar muscle 19
thirds 61, 70
thrown spiccato 26, 104
thumb **49**, 52, 62, 63, 78, 161
thumb connection 16
thumb position 54-55, **58**, 64
tone production 37
tone shape 71, 124
trills 96
tuning 85, **86**, 87
Twelve Lesson Course by K.
    Havas 3

unisons 69
upper arm 25, 26

vibrations **18**, 88
vibrato **66-68**
Vivaldi, A., music of
    E minor sonata 141-142

Wagner, Richard 110
Waldbauer, Imre iii
weight of bow 25
weight of 'cello **13**
weightlessness 14
wrist 26, 30, 150-151, 155
William Tell 125